# MEDIA CAREER GUIDE

## PREPARING FOR JOBS IN THE 21ST CENTURY

### THIRD EDITION

## JAMES SEGUIN

### ROBERT MORRIS COLLEGE

Bedford/St. Martin's

Boston ◆ New York

**For Bedford/St. Martin's**

*Communication Editor:* Jennifer Bartlett
*Developmental Editor:* Simon Glick
*Production Editor:* Maria Burwell
*Senior Production Supervisor:* Dennis Conroy
*Marketing Manager:* Richard Cadman
*Art Direction and Cover Design:* Lucy Krikorian
*Composition:* Publishing Synthesis, Ltd.
*Printing and Binding:* Malloy Lithographing, Inc.

*President:* Charles H. Christensen
*Editorial Director:* Joan E. Feinberg
*Publisher for History, Political Science, and Communication:* Patricia Rossi
*Director of Marketing:* Karen R. Melton
*Director of Editing, Design, and Production:* Marcia Cohen
*Managing Editor:* Erica T. Appel

*For information, write:* Bedford/St. Martin's, 75 Arlington Street, Boston, MA 02116
(617-399-4000)

ISBN: 0-312-39556-6

Very special thanks to Connie Serapiglia and Karen Zihmer for their invaluable assistance and support.

My thanks also to the Robert Morris College students who read and commented on the manuscript: Carri Clark, Jenn Marple, Greg Moorehead, Michael Theim and Misty Van Curen.

# CONTENTS

# INTRODUCTION

This guidebook is for college students majoring in the communications and media fields. As you get closer to graduation, it's natural to have questions about the types of jobs or careers that you can realistically look forward to. Competition is intense for the more desirable jobs in the communications fields. The good news is that Michigan State University's *Recruiting Trends 2000–2001,* a study that focuses solely on the hiring of college graduates, predicts a 19 percent increase for communications graduates when compared to 1999. Although this figure shows slightly slower growth than in previous years, there are many positive and exciting developments. I encourage you to look carefully at the Michigan State University's survey highlighted in Chapter 1, which projects a continued increase in jobs for those with a bachelor degree and particularly for those with a graduate degree in communications.

I believe this growth is occurring for two main reasons. The first is the Internet, which continues to transform how business is conducted. The Internet has pushed the already fast-growing computer related businesses into high gear. You may not see the connection between the careers of computer engineers, computer support specialists and desktop publishing specialists, and the careers of writers, editors or photographers, but take a moment to consider the larger trend. Whatever communications specialty you're interested in, you can be sure its growth is being fed by computer technologies. For communications majors, it's imperative to know how these computer technologies are changing your field and how you can graduate as a competent computer user. This requirement does not make technology more important than communications skills, creativity or ability to work in teams.

1

You still have to know your field well, but technology skills will help you communicate better. Another new emphasis I am seeing is that more is expected of graduates. You are expected to be well grounded in your major *and* have the necessary job-related skills upon graduation. Employers have always emphasized internships and job experience during college, but now these experiences are taking on greater importance than ever before. Savvy college students will take these trends to heart and build solid internships and jobs into their college years. It's common sense that such experiences can balance and enhance your classroom activities. When you begin interviewing for a job, you will immediately see their value.

The increased popularity of the Internet and computers is also the foundation for growth in what has become known as the *new media* field. Job growth in this field skyrocketed for a while, but is slowing in the early years of the new millennium. "New media" is a loosely defined term used to describe communications that are both created on and distributed through computers, Intranets and the Internet. New media encompasses a wide range of activities and occupations, including Web designers, writers and producers of interactive/multimedia presentations, editors of visuals and audio for streaming on the Web and so on. Fields such as desktop publishing, digital editing, public relations and independent filmmaking have many new media positions. They require competence in various software and design skills. It's best to see these jobs as bringing together both traditional media, such as video, and new media, such as video streaming. Another example is knowing traditional public relations activities as well as how to carry them out on the Internet. Again, you see the close bond between communications and computers. You can hardly say one without including the other. New media is the field putting it all together and you will find more information on it in Chapter 1.

The second reason for the increased demand of communications majors is that they are often well schooled in traditional communications skills. Even in this age of technological wonders, recruiters list traditional communications skills (writing, speaking, presenting and listening) as a close second to being well prepared in your discipline. This shouldn't be a surprise to anyone, but people act as if it is. Look around in your classes and at the places where you have worked or volunteered. Who rises to the top? Knowledgeable people who communicate well. Motivated people who communicate well. Communicating well is followed by several other important competencies: demonstrated ability to lead and work in teams, interpersonal and personal traits that have to do with motivation, honesty and work ethic.[1]

As the head of my own company, I have had the opportunity to hire young people right out of college and have seen some struggle and others excel. Why the difference? Surprisingly, it's pretty easy to pinpoint. My experience confirms the findings of the Michigan State survey. It's not just what you know about your field; employers are interested in a wide range of skills and personal attributes. Young people who have these skills or who are willing to develop them excel in the workplace. College is the perfect place to start. On the following pages, you will find suggestions about how to use your time in college to prepare yourself for entry into the job market. You will find detailed information about the high and low job growth areas, and you will find lists of industry trade magazines and contact information for professional organizations—all of which will help you stay current with the latest developments in your field, interact with other professionals and find job banks.

The tips provided cross several areas—practical things you can do, specialized reading and research, and a series of attitude checks that might require you to work on your interpersonal skills or attitudes toward work. Please don't think I am simply placing college in the category of vocational training—it's so much more than that, and I hope you agree. College is the time and place to broaden your knowledge and skills, develop strong values, learn about your strengths and weakness, and begin to see how you can contribute to a better society. Whether or not you have declared a major or decided on a career direction, the ideas on the following pages can help you further define what you would like to do—and be better at it.

---

[1]Adapted from *Recruiting Trends 2000–2001*. East Lansing: Collegiate Employment Research Institute, Michigan State University, 2001, p. 35. Used with permission.

# 1

# CONTEMPLATING A CAREER IN MEDIA/COMMUNICATIONS

The early years of the twenty-first century are fascinating times for people interested in communications and media. One indication is the AOL-Time Warner merger, forming the world's largest media conglomerate. The combination of Time Warner's traditional services and AOL's Internet leadership make the union symbolic. Is this the beginning of the end of old-line television, radio and print and the beginning of the truly digital media company? Many people think so. Then there is Napster, the online music-sharing business created by 19-year-old Shawn Fanning. He may have changed how the music industry distributes music and makes money. While his company may not survive, his innovation of peer-to-peer computing and free (or almost free) music on the Internet probably will. In the field of television, digital-TV is being phased in slowly, the networks continue to lose audience share and TV producers continue to search for new types of programming—hence the likes of TV series called *Survivor, Big Brother* and *Temptation Island.* But don't count on shows like these to reverse the trend in declining audiences. The perpetual media underdog, radio, is launching national satellite services and low-power FM stations and has consumers intrigued by Web radio. Radio is constantly being reinvented. If you're interested in print media, more than 800 magazines are started each year; while many fail, maga-

4

zines are targeting niche audiences more successfully than ever. News-paper readership is down, but newspaper Web sites are popular (al-though most are unprofitable).

One theme throughout all of these changes is that traditional work patterns are changing as well. For example, journalists are hired to write newspaper stories, report for the Web and appear on television news, whereas they used to write for just one medium. Creative people who for-merly specialized in videography are now expected to be acquainted with editing or producing. The times are not just fascinating; they are also challenging for many media professionals.

Considering recent developments, are media and communications industries good places to look for jobs or to hope for a career? With the disruptive influence of the Web, mergers and the productivity increases that stem from new technology, perhaps you are worried about your fu-ture. You don't need to be. Despite economic forces increasing compe-tition, most communications fields are growing, offering college gradu-ates a wide variety of opportunities. The stage was set for this growth about two decades ago when large media companies like CNN and MTV were founded. CNN was launched in 1979. MTV started in 1981 and, as you know, has had a worldwide impact on popular culture and all com-munications fields. These companies, along with advances in cable-TV, satellite communications, advertising and, of course, the Internet, have spurred the growth of jobs in a variety of fields employing writers, di-rectors, producers, public relations practitioners and advertising experts, to name a few. But they've also created spin-off jobs and products in re-lated media, such as books, magazines, films and video games. Where do you find jobs in these industries? Are they all off in some distant locale or can you find them in your own backyard?

Think about your possibilities from a regional perspective. Consider midsize cities such as Birmingham, Alabama; Toledo, Ohio; Boulder, Colorado or San Bernardino, California. Each city has numerous com-munications companies—from newspapers of various forms to televi-sion, cable and radio stations—and beyond that you will find dozens of communications suppliers—mostly small companies and freelancers who are creating communications for different purposes. If you look within a 50-mile radius of most any city, you will find that hundreds of communications firms exist—some thrive and some don't, but they are there competing for the communications business in that area. Go to smaller city markets and you will continue to find many communica-tions firms. They are everywhere, and many are doing more than adequate business. Whether the economy is on an up- or downswing, companies still need communications services.

How else can you get a sense of what media/communications opportunities exist? Consider one corporation in your area. It could be the size of a typical Fortune 500 company or a smaller high-tech company—either way, you can be sure there are departments within it producing communications that are used internally and others that are used outside the company. You can also be sure there is a bevy of small creative firms and freelancers providing communications services regularly for this company. If the company is growing, the communications services are growing, too. It doesn't matter what the company does—whether it is a manufacturer or a service company, whether it is privately owned or a subsidiary of another company—it must communicate to stay in business. Often such entities use a wide variety of communications and media to get their messages to target audiences. Companies are outsourcing (that is, hiring companies outside their own firms) for more of their communications work. This creates a dynamic and highly competitive market to supply services.

Typical firms producing corporate work include advertising and public relations, desktop publishing, technical writing, still photography, marketing, multimedia, new media, training and development and so on. As noted in the Introduction, the *Recruiting Trends 2000–2001*, published by the Collegiate Employment Research Institute of Michigan State University, indicates that communications majors are in demand (see Table 1.1). The study asked job recruiters who and what types of college graduates they expected to hire in the upcoming year. The most recent figures, the hiring expectations for 2001, were then compared with actual hiring in 2000. Between 2000 and 2001, the hiring of graduates with associate's, bachelor's and master's degrees in communications was expected to grow by 28 percent, 19 percent and 43 percent, respectively. The interest in master's degree candidates is significant. It sends a clear message from employers: "We want more experienced, more capable graduates."

The Michigan State University study focuses on the hiring of college graduates. You can get a sense of the marketplace from that study, but it's not enough in my opinion to understand the trends in the communications industries. It is interesting to look also at the growth of one communications specialty. The new media field is one of the most interesting to look at. A study completed by PricewaterhouseCoopers in March 2000 found that employment in the new media industry in the New York

**Table 1.1  AVERAGE NUMBER OF HIRES IN 1999–2000 AND EXPECTED IN 2000–2001 BY EVERYONE WHO RECRUITED AT LEAST ONE MAJOR FROM THESE CATEGORIES***

| Academic Major | Average Hires Made 1999–2000 | | Average Hires Expected 2000–2001 | | % Change |
|---|---|---|---|---|---|
| **All graduates** | | | | | |
| Business | (185) | 98.7 | (185) | 139.1 | +41 |
| Engineering | (188) | 76.2 | (192) | 121.1 | +59 |
| Computer Science | (12) | 92.1 | (119) | 174.1 | +89 |
| Liberal Arts | (44) | 64.9 | (43) | 92.4 | +42 |
| Science | (69) | 153.3 | (70) | 187.3 | +22 |
| Ag/Construction | (28) | 37.2 | (29) | 38.2 | +3 |
| Allied Health | (14) | 53.1 | (13) | 59.5 | +12 |
| *Communications* | *(33)* | *59.0* | *(33)* | *75.6* | *+28* |
| **Associates** | | | | | |
| Business | (50) | 7.7 | (48) | 9.3 | +21 |
| Engineering | (62) | 9.9 | (67) | 15.9 | +61 |
| Computer Science | (34) | 7.4 | (36) | 13.3 | +24 |
| Liberal Arts | (17) | 18.3 | (18) | 28.4 | +55 |
| Science | (18) | 19.7 | (19) | 20.5 | +4 |
| Ag/Construction | (5) | 1.0 | (7) | 1.0 | No Change |
| Allied Health | (2) | 20.0 | (2) | 19.0 | –5 |
| *Communications* | *(8)* | *7.2* | *(8)* | *9.1* | *+26* |
| **Bachelors** | | | | | |
| Business | (175) | 67.2 | (175) | 102.9 | +53 |
| Engineering | (174) | 47.0 | (180) | 75.7 | +61 |
| Computer Science | (112) | 68.8 | (112) | 130.6 | +90 |
| Liberal Arts | (40) | 46.8 | (42) | 62.1 | +33 |
| Science | (64) | 89.6 | (65) | 114.8 | +28 |
| Ag/Construction | (26) | 37.6 | (28) | 38.0 | +1 |
| Allied Health | (7) | 19.0 | (8) | 17.4 | –8 |
| *Communications* | *(30)* | *41.1* | *(30)* | *19.0* | *+19* |
| **Masters** | | | | | |
| Business | (76) | 18.7 | (72) | 25.0 | +34 |
| Engineering | (96) | 20.4 | (98) | 42.1 | +106 |
| Computer Science | (64) | 26.9 | (66) | 59.2 | +120 |
| Liberal Arts | (26) | 18.5 | (25) | 25.8 | +39 |
| Science | (32) | 19.1 | (29) | 22.0 | +15 |
| Ag/Construction | (8) | 7.1 | (9) | 4.0 | –44 |
| Allied Health | (1) | 25.0 | (1) | 25.0 | No Change |
| *Communications* | *(14)* | *3.7* | *(13)* | *5.3* | *+43* |

*Source:* Adapted from *Recruiting Trends 2000–2001* (East Lansing: Collegiate Employment Research Institute, Michigan State University, 2001), p. 33.

* Number in parenthesis refers to the number of respondents providing information.

City area alone increased by 40 percent between 1997 and 1999, to approximately 250,000 jobs. The total number of new media companies grew by 25 percent annually, to approximately 8,500 companies. While this fairly high rate of growth for new media companies and jobs is slowing down, the field of new media will nevertheless continue to strengthen. Look at the types of new media jobs in the following list. They require skill sets that combine design or creative skills with specific computer software competence. Since new media communications are created mostly on computers, graduates in this area have what so many employers are looking for. No matter where you look in the communications fields, employers have an insatiable need for graduates with technical expertise. Newspapers want graduates who understand journalism and Web technologies. Writers who know desktop publishing are in greater demand than those who don't. Competent video and television program editors who can use nonlinear editing systems are employable; those who do not will have trouble finding an editing job. To me, the new media field represents what is happening throughout the communications industries—a melding of traditional media skills with software competence or technical expertise. For many students, success in the job market will come because they developed communications and technical expertise while in college. If you are interested in the new media field, you might want to review the PricewaterhouseCoopers study, which is available at the Web site of the New York New Media Association at <http://www.nynma.org>. It's interesting to review the varied types of jobs identified in this survey:

**Content Design and Development**

Programming development for online/Internet services
Interactive advertising creative-design services
Design services for content providers
Title development for CD-ROMs, etc.
Film/video/animation services

**Content Packaging and Marketing**

Publishing/distribution of multimedia titles
Online/Internet services
Content distribution

**Electronic Commerce**

**Software Development**

**Content Creation Tools**
Audio recording
Design/illustration

**Enabling Services**
Marketing consulting
Design consulting
Technology consulting
Financial investment services

Suppose, however, that you're not interested in new media. Are there opportunities elsewhere? The following projections for specific communications occupations were compiled by the U.S. Bureau of Labor Statistics.[1] What types of communications jobs will have large or small increases in growth? For the period 1998–2008, the projections look like this:

**Fastest Growing (Increases 48–71 Percent)**
Desktop publishing specialists
Advertising, marketing, promotions, public relations and sales managers
Public relations specialists

**Faster-Than-Average Growth (Increases of 21–35 Percent)**
Actors, directors and producers
Various positions in cable-TV and other pay-television services
Photographers and camera operators
Writers (including technical writers) and editors

**Average Growth (Increases of 10–20 Percent)**
Designers (including set, lighting and costume), visual designers and
    commercial artists
Various positions in motion picture production and distribution
Photographers and camera operators for radio and television
Training and development specialists

---

[1]U.S. Bureau of Labor Statistics. *Occupational Outlook Handbook.* Washington, D.C.: Government Printing Office, 2001. Available at <http://www.bls.gov>.

**Slow Growth (Increases of 0–9 Percent)**

Advertising, marketing, promotions, public relations and sales managers for radio and television

News analysts, reporters, sportscasters, weathercasters and correspondents

Writers (including technical writers) and editors for radio and television

**Decline (Decreases of 1 Percent or More)**

Announcers for radio and television

Broadcast and sound technicians

Note that there is little growth expected in the radio and television fields. Even the high-growth jobs in public relations, for example, do not apply to radio and television station hiring. And the jobs so many students aspire to—on-camera positions such as sportscasters and weathercasters—show little growth also. New media positions are too new to be included in the Labor Bureau data. If they were included, however, you would see substantially higher growth in many new media occupations.

As these figures make clear, your preparation for entry into communications fields deserves careful thought. Some communications areas are growing rapidly, whereas others are declining. Take these factors into consideration in your job search. Also remember that even though the United States is the largest producer—and consumer—of communications in the world, there are exciting opportunities overseas, as American companies continue to expand into South America, Europe, Asia and beyond. The future for communications majors is bright.

# 2

# WHERE THE JOBS ARE

Students tend to consider too few opportunities. The opportunities abound, but many are tucked away under job categories that don't specifically belong to the traditional communications/media job market. Some additional categories to look for are often listed under corporate communications, education, new media, public information (government), training and development, satellite communications, video games/simulations and so on. Many of these jobs are similar to those in the traditional communications fields. Unless you widen your horizons, you eliminate at least half of the opportunities available to you before you even begin looking.

Following is a list of jobs that fall under the general heading of "communications fields"—and I'm sure there are more. I have divided them into traditional communications/media fields and related fields. The related fields are viable options. Please note that for some categories, where it is not clear which jobs might be included, I have listed the specialties that fall within that category.

## Traditional Communications/Media Fields
1. Advertising
2. Animation/Graphic Arts
3. Audio Production
4. Book Publishing
5. Commercials (Advertising) Production
6. Feature, Documentary and Independent Film Production
7. Magazine Publishing

8. Music/Recording Production
9. New Media/Multimedia/Interactive
10. Newspaper Publishing/Journalism
11. Public Relations
12. Radio
13. Television: broadcast and cable
14. Video Production
15. Writing

**Related Fields**

1. Arts/Theater Management
2. Captioning for the Hearing Impaired
3. Consulting
4. Institutional Communications (nonbroadcast): includes communications/media created by corporations, colleges/universities, government, military and nonprofit organizations
5. Internet, Online Related
6. Distribution and Duplication
7. Education: crisis communications, media training, teaching, conducting workshops and seminars
8. Equipment Manufacturers and Suppliers
9. Equipment and Business Brokers
10. Language Translation Services
11. Law: media and entertainment
12. Marketing and Sales
13. Media/Communications Facilities Design and Installation
14. Political Communications
15. Professional and Trade Organizations
16. Rides/Simulations: amusement parks, museums, science centers
17. Research: audience analysis, business, library, film, and video and film stock libraries
18. Satellite Related: direct broadcast satellite, video conferencing
19. Still Photography
20. Talent: actors, newscasters and weathercasters, on-camera spokespeople and voice-over narrators
21. Trade Magazines, Newsweeklies, Publications, Awards, Conferences and Marketplaces
22. Training and Development
23. Video Games

# 3

# STRATEGIES FOR SUCCESS: 33 TIPS TO PREPARE YOURSELF FOR A CAREER IN MEDIA/COMMUNICATIONS

In this chapter, I've listed 33 different tips you can use to prepare yourself better for a career in media/communications. As mentioned before, some of these suggestions require hands-on work, others require learning new skills and still others are more interpersonal. Of course, you're not going to be able use all of the tips, but find some that you can accomplish. Start slowly and build. One thing will lead to another. As your college years go by, your interests will change and become more specific, and all of a sudden you will feel that you are a lot closer to knowing what you want to do than you were six months before.

## GET STARTED

### 1. START CAREER PLANNING EARLY

It's reasonable to get started on career planning during your sophomore year. Consider your first year in college and the summer following it as a time of adjustment. After that, it's time to get a little more serious about career preparation—and each year afterward, a little more serious. It's okay to start slowly, and it doesn't matter if you have little idea of what you want to do. Everything suggested in this guidebook will help you focus your ideas and gain direction.

When you take action, unexpected things happen. For example, you may go to a bookstore to find a certain book, but instead you find a different book or run into someone who ends up helping you much more. These incidents occur frequently for those who keep trying. There is only one thing you don't want to do: nothing. That will delay your preparation and prevent you from developing your particular interests and passions—which, if you have none now, will come in time if you work at acquiring them. Without a strong area of interest and a developing devotion to it, you will not be motivated to learn more and seek out new experiences and opportunities. Early career planning is serious business, because out of these new learning opportunities and experiences—many of which come by chance—will come a direction that will shape your life after college. Awaiting you only a few years away may be a whole new set of friends, a much different location and job responsibilities that you can't imagine right now. Think about where you want to be, try to visualize your situation and then work toward it step by step. College is an engaging, mind-broadening learning experience. Make it pay off for you.

## 2. KEEP A NOTEBOOK/JOURNAL

I know a man who took an idea recorded in his notebook and turned it into a company now worth $3 billion. In high school he started writing down his ideas in a notebook. After college he used one of those ideas to start up an energy company that now employs about 17,000 people. You never know what things of future value you might be writing down in your own notebook of ideas, people, organizations, events or things that matter to you.

In addition to ideas, a notebook can help you keep track of what you are learning. After a year of making entries, you may find, when you look back through them, that you've forgotten about some important experiences. This points out one value of a journal: It helps you track your progress. This alone may boost your self-confidence and help you define a direction. Many college students tell me that they have no idea what they want to do. I suggest they keep a journal; it can be an incredible tool. A notebook can be the glue that holds different things together—for instance, the names of people you have met. These could be people who have visited your classes; people you've met on a field trip, summer job or internship; people you've encountered while visiting a classmate or attending a lecture series; someone you've read about. You should note a few things about each person and write down any available phone numbers, e-mail addresses and the like. The same holds true for organizations that impress you, places where you could perhaps see yourself working. Events you attend and books you read—these things qualify as well. What you note will probably depend on the time you have available and your motivation. If you make the time to keep a journal, you will find it to be more helpful than you can imagine.

## 3.  BE A CRITICAL CONSUMER

I was told that film director Steven Spielberg watched the movie *2001: A Space Odyssey* hundreds of times when he was a young man. I don't know if this is true, but think about it for a moment: watching one film over and over again until there is nothing else to learn from it. Have you ever done that? Did you ever like a song so much that you played it over and over again on a CD player, each time noticing new things about it and finding nuances you didn't catch at first? Media and communications go by us so rapidly in most cases that we don't have time to study them. Because of that, I'm encouraging you to try another approach—and it doesn't matter what communications field you're interested in. Find the best communications in your field, the ones recognized by the professional community as those of highest quality, and then study each one individually and in a concentrated fashion. Read, watch and listen to these communications again and again. Outline their structure, list their good and bad points. Keep a journal of what you are learning from them. Ask yourself why and how the authors or creators did what they did. How did they go about creating that communication? You may discover unexpected insights. If you find yourself lost, it's a clear indication of what you need to learn in your college coursework or on your own.

Another thing you can do—and it's very easy—is to pay special attention to current communications in your specialty. If your interest is in independent films and documentaries, for example, you should allow yourself enough time to watch them on HBO or wherever else they may appear. Often, you can find film festivals or independent film houses that show the kind of work you're interested in. You should know where they are and make a point to see what they're showing. If your interest is in advertising, you should consume and evaluate ads everywhere you see them—from billboards and magazines to electronic media and the Internet. There's so much advertising around us that you won't have to change your schedule—just start taking advantage of what you find naturally in your day-to-day activities.

Whether you follow up on any of this probably comes down to one question: How badly do you want to learn? Those who are hungry, driven or committed will take advantage of learning opportunities, and such efforts will pay off. Success takes drive, determination and a persistence that is hard to explain. These qualities, of course, will develop further when you go to work and stand face-to-face with the incredible demands and challenges of communications, but you have to prepare yourself now if you hope to be ready later on.

## 4. KEEP A FILE

Collect samples of communications that interest you. A simple accordion file—even a cardboard box—will work. It's easy to download newspaper articles from Internet sources, saving you the trouble of cutting and pasting and photocopying articles. Many movies, television shows, radio programs and CD-ROMs can be purchased. Press kits might be given to you by sponsoring organizations if you ask for them. Once you start keeping a file, find useful ways to categorize items for easy referral. Classroom projects, team projects and papers can often be enhanced by what you've collected in your file.

# LEARN ALL YOU CAN

## 5. BE A HISTORY BUFF

I can't stress enough the necessity of knowing as much about history as possible. What history? All history; it's hard to eliminate any areas or periods. Consider that good decisions are made in context. All aspects of communications work demand decision making—from creation to distribution—and decisions that bear fruit for an individual or a company are good for many reasons. Historical context is a tool to improve your decision making. The history of a community, a region, a company, an individual, a continent or an ethnic group can be helpful. For example, how could a journalist do a good job in

Bosnia if he or she did not know about previous conflicts and achievements of the people in that area? The same is true for many other fields. A Hollywood writer who submits a new quiz-show idea to a television network had better know the history of television quiz shows. Trying to accomplish communications work when you do not know the historical context will ultimately catch up with you.

Current events are history in the making, so keep up with them. If you do, you will be able to incorporate what you've learned into your classroom participation, your writing and eventually your on-the-job responsibilities. Let's say that one day you're asked to join a team assigned to develop a marketing plan for your company. The meetings are taking place in another part of the company, and when the team meets, you discover that you know no one. However, knowing current events will help you take part in informal conversation prior to the meeting and may even contribute to the development of the marketing plan. The point is this: Put in place now the activities that will help you land a good job and excel in it once you get there.

## 6. LEARN ABOUT COMPUTERS AND SOFTWARE

Computer technologies have become essential in all communications and media. You should know:

- How to use several types of software programs—word processing, presentation and spreadsheet.
- How to use e-mail to communicate with people inside and outside your organization. (You should know the e-mail commands well enough to be able to communicate with individuals and groups, forward mail and send attachments.)
- How to use the Internet for research.
- How to set up and edit a homepage on the Internet.
- How to load software and how to move around in applications on your company's menu of software.
- How to set up a workstation and get the cables in the right places.
- How to load and unjam the paper in a computer printer—and be willing to do so.

Computer literacy demands many skills and is absolutely critical to success today. If you are an intern or are employed now, you may find there are special applications for your business, such as marketing databases or project cost analyses. Become familiar with these immediately. If the company does not provide a training program, see if there is someone in the company who will get you started. Otherwise, get the operating manuals and learn what you can on your own. As a last resort, enroll in a vendor training program in order to learn the application. The cost of the program will be a smart investment in your future. In a larger sense, new technologies are often the reason for innovation and change in communications and media businesses. If you are not technically oriented, it is important not to let yourself be afraid of technology. Embrace new technologies as much as possible. Those who can ride the new waves of technology have a much better chance for employment and higher pay.

One way to enhance your computer expertise is to select information science, management information systems or information technology as a minor concentration during your college studies. The body of computer coursework has various names and subspecialties. If you have the interest and aptitude, it would be wise to consider a computer-related minor.

## 7. SPEAK THE TERMINOLOGY

Every business has its own terminology and acronyms. In many cases, this terminology is used liberally every day. It is important that you know and become comfortable using the terminology in regular conversation. Suppose you were on the first day of a new job and someone said to you:

"Roger, could you go to the supply room and get me three VHS cassettes, two metal BetaSPs and that old one-inch tape that's in the corner?"[1] (Television Commercial Production)

"Jan, we're going to have to do some quick research on these products . . . use one of the search engines on Bob's computer—I'll be right in." (Marketing or any field)

"Carol, your first assignment will be writing three PSAs[2] for Quality Corp. Here's some background to read before you go home tonight." (Public Relations)

---

[1] VHS, metal BetaSP and one-inch are videotape formats.
[2] PSA stands for "public service announcement."

Assuming that one of the preceding scenarios is related to your specialty, would you know what was being asked of you? If you are not familiar with the terminology used, look in the back of any textbook that covers basic communications industries for a glossary of terminology. There could easily be hundreds of terms. I suggest you learn the terminology well enough not only to pass a multiple-choice test but also to use the terms in business conversation.

## 8. BE A TEAM PLAYER

I don't know anyone who accomplishes communications work entirely alone. Perhaps a few people on the Internet or someone writing a small newsletter does so. Even famous novelists have editors and companies who market and sell their books. Indeed, teamwork is an accepted and essential way of accomplishing work; since you will live and die by the quality of the work that emanates from your team, you must be able to be a team player, which means (1) playing many different roles, (2) solving problems on the spot and (3) being assigned a task, working separately to accomplish it and then bringing it back to the team for evaluation and correction.

Diversity is a key characteristic of many successful teams. When you're on a team, particularly for the first time, look around to see what unique skills each person brings to the team. Ask yourself what *you* bring. Then go with your strengths and don't try to overextend yourself.

*Men, women, young, old, creative, technical, experienced, new-to-the-job*— these terms express the diversity you are likely to find on a team. Diverse perspectives expand the range of ideas considered, then act as checks and balances in sifting out less-effective approaches.

### Listening/Observing/Thinking/Brainstorming

These highly focused and energy-consuming activities are the foundation of good teamwork. Without them you can't fully understand the mission of the team or the expected work flow. Make sure you understand the parameters of typical brainstorming sessions: You are working in a judgment-free environment in which all ideas are welcome. Evaluation and organization of those ideas follow.

### Making Contributions

Active participation is essential. Sitting there like a bump on a log will not do. Contributions mean preparation. If that means burning the midnight oil or arriving an hour before everyone else, do it. Newcomers should contribute carefully at first and only after the seasoned veterans have set the pace. Look for areas where you can offer to do extra work or solve a problem. That's one way to establish a solid, hard-working reputation and at the same time help drive a project to completion.

### Controlling Emotions

Exuberance is desirable, but anger, bitterness or criticism of others in a group situation can be very damaging. Making negative comments about fellow employees is off-limits. Badmouthing someone will mean that you, too, will become a target of criticism. If you can be a positive force, you will be recognized as an outstanding contributor and a valuable employee. People will begin to trust you. Maintaining a positive energy in the workplace is a key ingredient of success.

### Problem Solving

What problems need to be solved? Find a way to solve the ones that are appropriate for you. If that means delivering things, researching, coordinating by making phone calls and assisting in the preparation of presentations—offer to do them. By doing such things, you're showing that you understand the pressure of deadlines and the need for productivity.

### Be Willing to Compromise

Learn the art of compromise. It's not easy, but it's essential if a team is to be productive.

## 9. READ WHAT THE PROS READ

You already have textbooks and related readings assigned for coursework. Read and absorb those with a passion. In addition, I'm suggesting something a little different: that you begin to read what communications and media professionals read to keep up on current events and developments in their industries. Industry surveys of communications executives have found that managers stay abreast of key developments in their industries through three methods:

1. Reading industry publications
2. Attending industry conferences and seminars
3. Networking—that is, meeting and interacting with others

Reading, attending conferences and networking all help managers gather information, evaluate it and (one hopes) make better decisions—ranging from what equipment to buy, who to hire, who to align themselves with, what new products or services to launch, how to satisfy customers better, how much risk to take, whether to borrow money or not and so on. All these decisions must be based on solid ground. Fortunes and careers depend on good decision making. Reading is one way to decrease risk and increase the chances of success.

Once you start reading, it won't be long before you realize how valuable it is. Most any publication will have a few pertinent articles in your field of study. As you read over a period of just one week, you will begin seeing connections and following significant mergers or new product launches. As you read over a longer period of time, you will start noting the people, trends and organizations that are mentioned often.

Of course, you're not going to be able to read every publication listed here. To help you get started, I have reviewed (and, in some cases, provided headlines and examples from) representative articles from some of the publications listed to give you an idea of the types of articles you will find as you read. Begin slowly. Learn to skim to find the most important articles for your purposes—then read those. Most publications suggested here are available free in your college or public library or can be accessed on the Internet. Following the recommended readings list is a more detailed explanation of the types of information contained in many of the publications.

## Recommended Readings

Choose from the following lists of newspapers, business magazines, and industry trade publications:

### Newspapers

*Baltimore Sun*
*Boston Globe*
*Chicago Tribune*
*Christian Science Monitor*
*Los Angeles Times*
*New York Times*
*Philadelphia Inquirer*
*St. Petersburg Times*
*USA Today*
*Wall Street Journal*
*Washington Post*
Local newspaper
Local business newsweekly

**Business Magazines**
*Business Week*
*Forbes*
*Fortune*
*U.S. News & World Report*

**Industry Trade and Specialty Publications**
(Depending on your area of specialization)
*Advertising Age*
*AV Video & Multimedia Producer*
*Billboard*
*Broadcasting & Cable*
*Business Marketing*
*Hollywood Reporter*
*INFOWORLD*
*Interactive Week*
*International Satellite Business Journal*
*INTERNETWEEK*
*Marketing News*
*NewMedia*
*Radio World*
*Shoot*
*Television Broadcast*
*Training*
*Variety*
*Videography*

**Other Publications**

Consider *Newsweek* to *Rolling Stone* to whatever interests you. In addition, I highly recommend *Brill's Content,* which covers the media with a decidedly critical eye. Published by Stephen Brill, who is also known for starting *Court TV* and *American Lawyer Magazine,* the publication highlights how the media covers events and often asks whether reporting is biased and comprehensive. Recent articles have considered whether the Pulitzer Prize, journalism's top honor, is awarded in a fair manner, how well the media covered the 2000 presidential campaign, a behind-the-scenes look at *George* magazine, and how a reporter for the *Los Angeles Times* influenced the Federal Drug Administration to remove a diabetes drug from the market. Other items of interest in

*Brill's Content* have included contributions by famous media critics, such as David Halberstram, and frequent articles on new media, such as an article on how the internet company, DoubleClick, is defending its privacy policy.

Let's take a closer look at some of the publications in the recommended readings list. What can you expect to find in these publications that will advance your education and career opportunities?

## 1. Newspapers

There are at least six newspapers you should become familiar with. If these don't interest you, consider some of the other newspapers in the preceding list.

***Wall Street Journal*** (<http://public.wsj.com>). The *Wall Street Journal (WSJ)* is not only for business majors and working business professionals. Many communications professionals also read the *WSJ* daily and use it as one of their primary sources of information—information on which they base important decisions. Your first step is to get a current issue and look it over. Here are some helpful hints.

The six columns on the front page of the *WSJ* are an incredible resource and include articles on most aspects of business, including human interest articles with a business angle. Two columns are devoted to "What's News." This section, divided into "Business and Finance" and "World Wide," provides summaries of the day's news with references to the articles within the paper. If you read nothing else, this section alone will help you. In "Today's Contents" you will find articles listed by topic—"Media," "Advertising," "Travel and Leisure," etc.—and special sections such as "Corporate Focus," "Industry Focus" and "Weekend Report." When the *WSJ* runs a special section on technology or health and medicine, it provides in-depth coverage of news, trends, people, companies and analysis. You learn a lot quickly by reading these sections. The *WSJ* has two other sections, "Market Place" and "Money and Investing": "Market Place" has plenty of articles on the media, focusing on different media at different times, whereas "Money and Investing" will probably only interest those of you with stocks and investments.

In a typical edition of the *WSJ*, I often find headlines crossing several media topics, including telecommunications, advertising, cable and broadcasting. For example:

*Special Report on Telecommunications (25 pages)*: "It's War! Telecom Battle Turns Into a Free-for-All," "Calling on the Internet" and "Cable Giants Fight Back"

*Advertising:* "Philip Morris Starts Lifestyle Magazine"

*Broadcasting:* "Hell Hath No Fury Like a Talk-Show Host"

*Who's News:* "Sony, Hoping to Restore Stability, Names Lucy Fisher to Oversee Columbia TriStar"

The Special Report on Telecommunications and the other three articles may or may not be of specific interest to you. But if the articles in today's issue do not interest you, the ones in tomorrow's may. In addition, by reading the *WSJ* you will learn about business trends and new developments. By reading the classified ads you will see what types of jobs are in demand. And don't forget to read the other ads—for the most part, they're excellent examples of communication, and they can tell you whether a company or industry is on the upswing or downswing. A fee is required to read the *WSJ* online.

**National Newspapers.**  Another newspaper to put on your list is a national newspaper such as the *New York Times,* the *Christian Science Monitor,* the *Washington Post,* the *Chicago Tribune* or the *Los Angeles Times.* Let's first look at one issue of the *New York Times.*

The Monday issue of the *New York Times* devotes the business section to the information industries. Often the entire section is relevant to media and communications majors because many information companies—particularly those involved in computer-related hardware, software and data services—seem to be merging or working together with communications companies. In the two Monday sections I reviewed, there were several articles of interest, as you can tell from the following sampling of headlines:

"On-line Magazine ('Slate' by Microsoft) Delays Charging a Fee"
"Sports Service Battles N.B.A. in Round Two" (This article is about a pager that gives immediate scores of the New York Knicks games, basket by basket.)
"Advertising" (This article describes some of the major advertising accounts that changed hands that week, particularly at the famous Leo Burnett Agency in Chicago.)

"European TV" (This article has a dateline of Cologne, Germany.) "Wooing Internet Gamers" (This article lists five companies that are developing online games predicting fast growth in this area.)

Two other articles of interest were also found in the same issues. One describes the audio and video standards being developed for the Internet so that companies can better compete with broadcasters. The other, in the "Media" section, reports on how movie companies track opening revenues on weekends and use that information to make decisions about future advertising and marketing plans.

You can see the wide range of topics covered in just two issues of the *New Yoirk Times*. Again, make sure to read the advertisements. One ad that I read states that revolution is not on television, but on the World Wide Web. It is an entertainment revolution, and the ad directs readers to Web-shows like "The Spot" (the original cybersoap), "EON-4" (a sci-fi thriller) and "The Pyramid" (a twisted corporate drama). This advertisement is sponsored by American Cybercasting with the caption, "The Origin of Internet Entertainment." Interested students who will soon be job seekers should hop on the Web and familiarize themselves with these new entertainment products.

Much can be learned by investing a few minutes in reading relevant articles. Consider, for example, a two-column article by Robin Pogrebin, from the "Media" section of the *New York Times*. Its subject is publishing; the author summarizes a trip to Bermuda to cover the American Magazine Conference. The article is loaded with information that any aspiring magazine writer or future editor needs to know: (1) the business outlook—it's good, according to this writer; (2) two national organizations—Magazine Publishers of America, and the American Society of Magazine Editors; (3) the name of the national conference and its sponsor—the American Magazine Conference; (4) the name of a handbook—*Guide to New Consumer Magazines,* by Samir Husnu; (5) the names of several important people in the industry and the companies that employ them; (6) a quote from Michael Eisner, president of Walt Disney Company, who was the main speaker at the conference; and (7) interesting statistics, such as: Although the total number of ad pages has decreased, the amount magazines are earning for each page has increased; total magazine ad revenues are up moderately. This one article is a gold mine for those whose eyes are on the magazine industry. The *New York Times* Web site( <http://www.nytimes.com>) is free, but requires registration. It's a wonderful site, particularly if you're interested in coverage of the media and the Internet.

*Christian Science Monitor* (<http://www.csmonitor.com>).   In addition to the standard sections—"World," "USA," "News in Brief," and editorials—the *Christian Science Monitor* has wonderful articles on "Arts & Leisure," "Learning," "Homefront," "Ideas," "Travel," "Books," "About Kids" and "Cybercoverage." I find things in the *Monitor* that I don't find in other papers. The Web site is very easy to use and pleasing to the eye. The "Learning" section on the Web has five or six articles to choose from, as do the other online sections.

*USA Today* (<http://www.usatoday.com>).   This national daily provides frequent coverage of media and communications issues and developments in its four major sections: "Newsline," "Moneyline," "Sportsline" and "Lifeline." The articles are brief and easy to read. "Newsline" and "Lifeline" often have lead stories about pop culture and media; these sections seem to be the favorites among the paper's readers. "Sportsline" includes articles about sports television that offer a critique of television sports coverage and tell of new developments, such as plans for new sports channels. *USA Today* is a good place to start your reading; you can then expand from there as you become more knowledgeable and develop focused interests. The paper's Web site is colorful and fun to use.

**Local Newspaper.**   You should read this type of paper so that you are knowledgeable about local events. If your goal is to work in the local job market, the local paper should be high on your reading list.

**Local Business Newspaper.**   Many midsize cities (and, of course, the larger ones) publish at least one business newsweekly. In addition to the articles that cover most industries in an area, these papers have a special focus each week, sometimes taking an in-depth look at one industry or topic. A local business paper can be an invaluable resource about people and firms in your area. In a focus on advertising, the paper may list all the agencies in the area, with key personnel, addresses, phone numbers and the like. These newsweeklies also publish related resource guides. For example, the *Pittsburgh Business Times* publishes the "Book of Lists," which lists area businesses by type. This is incredibly useful because it is the kind of information you'll need in order to write or call companies you're interested in. You will also be able to see how local firms differ in terms of gross sales, number of employees and so on—with all of this data in one book. Local business papers also provide a comprehensive record of activities that are important in the marketplace. For example, the "Record" section of the *Pittsburgh Business Times* has sixteen different listings, noting new incorporations, a calendar of events, Internet addresses and so on.

## 2. Business and General Interest Magazines

You have many choices here. Business magazines provide in-depth coverage of most communications and media topics. Magazines such as *Business Week, Forbes, Fortune* and *U.S. News & World Report* are good reading. Let's take a quick look at the two issues of *Business Week* I have in front of me.

**Business Week** (<http://www.businessweek.com>). One issue has the cover story, "Cable-TV Crunch: New Technologies Threaten Old-Line Operators." It's a four-page article summarizing the current problems of cable-TV. It's a quick read, providing statistics, analysis of the problems and profiles of key players. You can learn a great deal by taking ten minutes to read the article. If your career objectives include cable-TV, the article is obviously of interest, but those in advertising, marketing and public relations can also benefit.

On the cover of the other issue is the following: "Marketing—Make It Simple: Marketers Sell Too Much Stuff in Too Many Different Ways. Now the Smart Ones Are Cutting the Complexity. Once Again, P&G Is Leading the Charge." This is also a four-page story with great graphics, photos and sidebars. The article highlights a current trend. Sidebars explain key parts of P&G's strategy to pare down; another sidebar lists what Toyota, Nabisco, Citibank, General Motors and others are doing in the same vein. Key people are highlighted.

There is a follow-up article of interest to both advertising and marketing majors. The headline of this one-page article about a famous advertising executive reads, "Maurice Saatchi: The Flash Is Back, but . . . Despite Some High-Profile Clients, His New Firm Is Scrambling." What more could you ask for? By reading articles like this, you basically have professionals doing research for you. The writers have a byline, so you can e-mail or call them with your questions.

Another advantage of this type of reading is that it familiarizes you with the terminology commonly used in the industry, terminology you may first hear in the college classroom. Your reading is proof of how important the terms are in real business situations.

The articles that appear frequently in most business publications about computers and information processing may be useful background for everyone, since computers are important to most businesses and individuals. And don't forget to read the book reviews, editorials and (again) advertisements. You can learn from all these sections.

Another thing I like about magazines such as *Business Week* is that the table of contents is typically so well organized and easy to read that you can quickly select articles of interest to you. Subheadings such as "International Business," "Marketing," "Information Processing," "Science & Technology" and "Personal Business" lead you to sections that carry articles about media and communications.

General interest and newsmagazines are also worth reviewing. *Time* and *Newsweek*, for example, provide summaries of international events and issues. Read whatever magazines you find of interest, and keep reading them. Cultivate your own interests. A good way to expand your knowledge of the magazines that are available is to browse through the magazine section of your college library. Often the magazines are displayed so that you can see fifty or more current issues at a glance. In these displays, you'll probably find magazines that you didn't even know existed. When I visit the magazine section of my library, I often find magazine cover stories about projects I am currently working on. You may have the same experience, finding articles that help you with a class project.

The Web sites for the other business magazines in the recommended readings list are also worth browsing:

*Forbes*                              http://www.forbes.com

*Fortune*                             http://www.fortune.com

*U.S. News & World Report*            http://www.usnews.com

### 3. Industry Trade and Specialty Publications

This is an extremely important type of reading, and once you get involved in a specific communications field, it may be the most important reading you do. In my experience, college students do not read these types of publications and often don't even know they're available. These are the publications that working professionals read. Most trade publications now have Internet addresses and online versions. There are far too many trade publications to review in this brief guidebook. I have highlighted several in the following discussion and noted their Web addresses also. In most cases, the online versions for these magazines are well worth getting familiar with. Many are free or have some parts that you do not have to pay for. However, if these are not appropriate for you, talk with your professors, advisors, librarians and the working professionals you meet for suggestions on what you should read.

*Advertising Age* (<http://www.adage.com>). This publication is essential reading for anyone interested in advertising, public relations, direct mail and commercial production. Moreover, there are special issues focusing on the broadcasting, newspaper or magazine industries. *Advertising Age* is well written and designed so that almost everyone will find it fascinating. It is recommended reading no matter what your field of study. The issue I have before me has dozens of articles that interest me. Here are some examples of the headlines:

"Lexus Tries E-mail for Auto Intro"
"Children Tuning out TV in Alarming Numbers"
"Blockbuster to Co-Brand Video and Music Outlets"
"Reebok Spots Tip-off New League: Sponsor of Women's Basketball
    Plans TV, Print & Radio Ads"

When you start reading a new publication, notice how it is structured. *Advertising Age* is divided into sections by media. If you are looking for an article on a particular topic in advertising or public relations, try thumbing through several copies of *Advertising Age*. This will take you on a great trip, and you may find exactly what you want or new topics that you would not have found had you searched a reference work such as the *Readers' Guide to Periodical Literature*. Sometimes when I'm reading a publication like *Advertising Age*, I get so absorbed in the articles that I forget how much time I'm spending. Resources like the *Readers' Guide* will help with most research needs, but they can't provide you with references from current issues. In addition, *Advertising Age* does a wonderful job with special topics such as health care, magazines, radio and so on. If you happen to come across a special topic in *Advertising Age* related to a project you are working on, you will probably find a wealth of helpful information within it. As I suggested in the earlier section on newspapers, take careful note of the advertising. Ask yourself, "Who is advertising?" "What do I think of the ads?" These are questions worth considering. After you have evaluated the ads, scan the classified ads, the business-to-business sections and the want ads. Other advertising trade publications include *Adweek, Journal of Advertising* and *Journal of Advertising Research.*

*AV Video & Multimedia Producer* (<http://www.avvmmp.com>). This is a monthly publication for those involved in corporate training, industrial videos, event and meeting planning, trade shows and related fields. There is an emphasis on subjects directed toward interactive multimedia producers. Cover stories are typically about nonlinear-editing systems, in-house video facilities planning, video conferencing and interactive training products.

*AV Video & Multimedia Producer* examines projects and issues from a producer's or project manager's point of view. In this sense, it is a highly focused and useful publication. It is read by more than 100,000 senior producers and team leaders.

This magazine has a very handy "Yellow Pages" section in the back that lists company names, addresses, phone numbers and e-mail addresses for all the products and services mentioned or advertised in the issue. Most other magazines include a similar but less comprehensive listing.

*Billboard: The International Newsweekly of Music, Video and Home Entertainment* (<http://www.billboard.com>). *Billboard,* a thoroughly entertaining publication that focuses mostly on the music and music-video businesses, is considered the bible of the music industry. Its music coverage spans creative, technical and business subjects. The front page is devoted to news; following that you will find sections on "Artists and Music," "International," "Merchants and Marketing," "Reviews and Previews," "Programming," "Classified Advertising," "Real Estate" and so on. Also included are sections on music genres, such as "R&B," "Dance" and "Rap," as well as feature articles, editorials and charts detailing the gross sales of albums, singles and videos. Here are a few headlines that might tweak your interest:

"Can Superdweeb Save Network Biz?"
"Hootie's 'I Go Blind' May Be a Hit, but It's Also a Mixed Blessing"
"Bob Marley Album Hits 'Legendary' Heights"

Like many other industry trade publications, *Billboard* has great special-focus issues and a wonderful "The Year in Music" issue, published annually in December. It would be difficult to overestimate the value of the encyclopedic nature of this newsmagazine. Those who want to know what's going on in the music industry need to read *Billboard*. The "Executive Round Table" section provides names and pictures of key people moving to new jobs or projects. And the articles are filled with names of people who hire new employees. Other music publications to be familiar with are *Rolling Stone, Spin* and *Vibes*.

***Broadcasting & Cable: The Newsweekly of TV, Radio & Interactive Media.*** (<http://www.broadcastingcable.com>).   This popular publication is read throughout the television, cable, radio, multimedia, entertainment and media-law fields. In the issue I have before me, the cover story is about the digital-TV standard. Inside, "Fast Track" covers top stories of the week; one story is about declining network TV share, another about Howard Stern and a third about an important decision by the Federal Communications Commission (FCC). "Broadcasting," "Cable" and "Technology" sections highlight such subjects as TV violence, Hispanic stations and new technology that MSNBC (the joint venture of Microsoft and NBC) plans to use. You can see how topical and diverse the coverage is—essential reading for those who want to be in the know.

***Business Marketing: The Newspaper of Business-to-Business Marketing.*** (<http://www.businessmarketing.com>).   This is a publication of Crain Communications, the company that also publishes *Advertising Age*. *Business Marketing* is an excellent publication with some of the design pizzazz of *Advertising Age*. Remember, it focuses on business-to-business marketing, a very important segment of the marketing industry, but it seems less well known by college students. *Business Marketing* includes a range of articles, such as:

"Video Conferencing Adds Speed and Saves Dollars"
"Business-to-Business Snags $51.7 Billion"
"Industry Spotlight—Enterprise/Networking: Growth of Networks
    Heightens Reseller Role"
"Editorial: Ignoring Web's Marketing Potential Is a Huge Mistake"

*Business Marketing* has easy-to-read, colorful graphics and great ads. The online version, called *BtoB. The Magazine for Marketing and E-Commerce Strategies,* provides both articles and resources, including a directory of portals, a Web development directory and profiles of companies known for their effective marketing and advertising strategies.

*Hollywood Reporter* (<http://www.hollywoodreporter.com>). This is a "must read" for anyone interested in the feature-film and network-television industries. It gives the inside word on current and upcoming projects and the people involved. It also covers key issues like copyright and the Internet or special features on the Academy Awards. Because the *Hollywood Reporter* is expensive, many libraries do not subscribe to it.

*INFOWORLD: Defining Technology for Business* (<http://www.infoworld.com>). This publication is directed to the business-minded person who has an interest in communications. *INFOWORLD* includes a varied mix of articles and topics. One issue, for example, covers state-of-the-art media used for training, analyzes legislation affecting information and Internet businesses, discusses privacy concerns with the FCC's ruling on 911 numbers for cell phones and provides a useful section on management and careers.

*Interactive Week* (<http://www.zdnet.com/intweek/>). You need to know as much about the Internet as you can, particularly developments affecting media/communications. If you read just the "Newsfront" section of this slick Ziff-Davis publication, you will be pretty well informed. One issue I reviewed covers the growth of Charter Communications, a cable company; Disney's launch of its "Broadcast Center" on Infoseek's Go Network; administrative changes at WebTV; and new strategies at Warner Bros. Online Networks. Also mentioned in the same issue are recent activities at Yahoo!, Cnet, NBC, RealNetworks and Microsoft. Once you register, by providing the name of your place of employment and job title, you may qualify to receive this publication free of charge.

*International Satellite Business Journal.* Established in 1977, this journal is written for decisionmakers in the international arena. It is published by Intertec Publishing and has offices in Colorado, Washington and Kansas as well as in Japan, Italy and France. It has a typical structure: a front section with news and analysis followed by several in-depth articles. The articles in one issue include profiles of the emerging satellite services in Africa; Galaxy's Latin American distance education initiative; and a profile of Noah Samara, chairman and CEO of World Space, Inc., a company planning to offer digital radio programming to consumers in Africa, Asia and Latin America. The back section has a useful marketplace for advertisers but no job listings.

Another satellite publication to take note of is *Via Satellite*, which covers a wide range of topics. The articles in one issue discuss satellites and the Internet, satellites in the booming Japanese market, new mobile satellite technologies and the global launch industry. The magazine also publishes the annual *Profiles: A Strategic Planning and Resource Guide,* in which companies profile their services and achievements over the past year.

*INTERNETWEEK* (<http://www.internetweek.com>). This publication has an e-commerce emphasis and often covers advertising, marketing and media as they relate to Internet businesses. It commonly covers net infrastructure and wireless technologies news. In addition, *INTER-NETWEEK* provides in-depth articles on such subjects as satellites and bandwidth as well as reviews of new products and services. This magazine is especially useful to entrepreneurs and new media professionals.

*Marketing News: Reporting on the Marketing Profession* (<http://www.ama.org/pubs/>). This biweekly business publication of the American Marketing Association is a hybrid newspaper/magazine containing only fourteen to fifteen pages of articles in each issue. Although *Marketing News* is not flashy, it does provide a wide variety of articles and a good "Marketplace" section for job hunters and service providers.

*NewMedia* (<http://www.newmedia.com>). If your interests include both video and Web design, *NewMedia* could be the most useful publication for you. Published monthly, it often reviews products like Web-publishing systems or DVD-video authoring. Features highlight developments—for example, in interactive TV—or analyze distribution of music over the Internet. The articles are informative, well researched and concise. *NewMedia* is targeted to new media professionals, but it is appropriate for any media student or professional who wants to stay current with digital technologies.

*Radio World: Radio's Best-Read Newspaper* (<http://www.radioworld.com>). This newsmagazine is published biweekly. It provides straightforward and thorough coverage of radio business deals, feature stories on organizations and people, technology updates, employment listings and (sometimes) a buyer's guide. If you are interested in radio, this is a good periodical to get you started.

*Shoot: The Leading Newsweekly for Commercial Production and Postproduction.* This is a fascinating newsweekly targeted to the producers and directors of television commercials. It focuses on people (particularly directors), and companies that assemble the crews and supply equipment for production and postproduction of commercials. It has brief, promotion-like articles and copious, splashy ads promoting top directors, graphics firms, and postproduction and duplication houses. It also carries editorials.

*Shoot* is directed to those who shoot film and tape. Back sections include "Personnel Pool," "Production Services," "Street Talk," "Rep Report" and "Bulletin Board." Because these sections are short and in the back, they can easily be overlooked—but they can tell you a great deal. In "Personnel Pool" you can see the types of people who are in demand, or you can advertise your own services. "Production Services" may indicate which facilities are busy and therefore possibilities for internships or jobs. "Rep Report" and "Street Talk" focus on people who are moving to new jobs, or firms that are expanding or starting up. "Bulletin Board" is very important—it lists the dates of conferences and seminars of interest to those involved in commercial production. While most of these events are held in New York, Los Angeles, London and other large markets, if you read often enough, you will be sure to find conferences that are held in other parts of the country. Attending conferences during college will greatly enhance your education and readiness for the job market.

*Television Broadcast: The Technology Newsmagazine for Management, Engineering, Operations and Production* (<http://www.TVBroadcast.com>). This is a monthly newsmagazine with brief articles and a punchy style that highlights newscasting. You will find summaries of industry surveys on equipment purchases, newsroom organization, technology systems for enhancing productivity and new graphic weather systems like Storm Tracker. *Television Broadcast* is an excellent resource for those in the television news business. A separate Web site (<http://www.DigitalTelevision.com>) focuses on digital-TV issues.

*Training: The Human Side of Business* (<http://www.astd.org>).   This publication is not one you would normally find in a guidebook on media and communications, but those who are interested in corporate communications—and, of course, those looking toward the training and development field—should be familiar with this monthly magazine. So much of training and development work depends on communications and the use of various forms of media that it could be an attractive area for students to consider. This is a slick, well-written magazine. One issue includes an industry report analyzing how and where corporate America spent $59.8 billion in formal training. A chart shows the percentage of companies that use instructional methods and media. A few highlights: Videotapes are used by 79 percent, audio cassettes by 46 percent, games and simulations by 39 percent and computer-based training and multimedia by 37 percent. This is a vibrant, growing industry that is appropriate for communications and media majors.

*Variety: The International Entertainment Weekly* (http://www.variety.com>). If you're interested in the world of feature films or network television, *Variety* is worth reading regularly. Also covered are independent filmmakers, national cable programmers, syndicators and distributors—the business that emanates from Hollywood and New York. *Variety* is famous for its hip writing style. Like *Billboard*, it's fun to read. A few headlines will give you an idea of the weekly's style:

"Hare-y Issue: Who Conceived Jordan's Jam?"
"ABC Cashes Carey as Web Whirls Wednesday"
"Talking Small, Spending Big: Although Some Studio Execs Talk
   About Cutbacks, Hollywood Is Gearing up for Still More Movies &
   Bigger Star Salaries"
"Telecom Act's Bad Line"

*Variety* tracks the gross receipts of the movie industry. It also has a section on theater entitled "Legit." Again, the value is that you get not only the inside view but also the names of people starting new jobs and new ventures. In one article, "Fox Restructures Programming Arm," both the Vice President of Current Programming and the Director of Comedy Development are mentioned. A student interested in working in television programming would be wise to keep a copy of the article and record the names of key people in a notebook for future reference.

*Videography: The Magazine of Professional Video Production, Technology, and Applications* (http://www.videography.com>). This is a very good monthly publication for those who are interested in video production and postproduction, uses of computers in video, new developments in equipment (such as digital cameras, lighting, graphics and animation) and international production. It is directed mainly toward the producer of nonbroadcast communications and is read extensively by the wide variety of creative, technical and managerial professionals who produce this kind of work.

These are a few of the valuable industry trade and specialty publications. Look for the ones in your specialty, and try to read at least one regularly. Don't be afraid to browse. If you don't have time to read one in depth, at least skim through the articles to try to keep abreast of current events in your chosen industry.

## 10. BECOME OTHER-CENTERED

This is a very important career idea, and it can open doors that might otherwise remain closed. Let's say that you are assigned the job of developing communications to help people prepare their federal income taxes. It doesn't matter whether you're interested in the topic. A communications job must be designed to meet the mission established by clients or supervisors. These people pay and evaluate you. In most cases, the role of a communicator is to find a way to connect with other people—the target audience for a communication. The specific goals will vary depending on whether the purpose of the communication is to inform, persuade, motivate, entertain or sell. But the general goal—connecting—is always the same. Therefore, your ability to understand what motivates your audience, to be empathic, is critical. The better you can do this, the better communications you will create.

Another part of being other-centered is to recognize how your contributions are an essential part of your team's work. By doing your part well, you make others look good. It's a simple matter to see that the effort pays off for everyone, including yourself. This approach even extends to doing the "little extra things." For example, suppose a project has been completed late, yet it must reach the client the next day. Your project team has missed all overnight pickups from UPS, Federal Express and so on. It occurs to you that the package could be driven to the Federal Express office and still go out that night. What to do? You volunteer to get it there. When you do something like this, you have entered a new realm of being helpful and other-centered. You have visibly demonstrated that you recognize how important it is to the business and to this particular team to meet the deadline. You have also demonstrated that the time of the people you're working with is valuable and that you are willing to go the extra mile. It won't be forgotten.

It's easy in the college-student world to overlook the fact that communications are made for profit. Hardly anyone makes communications for themselves—they're too expensive and complex for individuals to produce in most cases. They're made to meet the goals of others—the more you can look at problems and solutions from another's point of view, the better job you can do. This is one of the most difficult tasks in developing communications.

## 11. LEARN ABOUT COMPANY BUDGETS

This takes time. Your college coursework can help with this, particularly upper-level courses, but often colleges don't teach you the attitude toward money and budgets that exists in communications businesses. Communications businesses make money in very specific ways: for example, by charging for employees' time, by charging fees for licensing a product, by collecting commissions when purchasing advertising time and by selling advertising time. There are also flat fees for creating products, writing proposals and so on. Overhead and profit are built into or added on to these fees. In most cases, communications businesses are labor-intensive and complicated. Small mistakes in budgeting may wipe out the profit or even turn a project into a money loser. Not knowing the ins and outs of how your firm budgets is a big mistake. Built into the rates and charges of communication companies are assumptions about the time it takes to accomplish something, appropriate delivery systems and proper return on investment. All of this means that going over budget or failing to keep track of costs can be dangerous. If you are involved in or responsible for even a small part of a budget, anything out of the ordinary should be discussed with your supervisor. Open communication is important, as is demonstrating a healthy respect for profit.

## 12. LEARN HOW TO MAKE COFFEE AND ACTUALLY MAKE IT

Traditionally, there are three survival skills often mentioned by teachers to students: Swim, use a computer and drive a stick shift (you still need to know how). I'll add a fourth—know how to make coffee. Many college students don't drink coffee, but most working professionals do—and not much happens in the morning until the coffee's been made. If you are serving an internship and see a harried professional making coffee every morning, you could make yourself famous in an instant. Offer to make the coffee and then do it every day. Have you simply shown an amazing sensitivity by making coffee? No. You've gone one better. You've shown that you recognize that the professional's time is valuable. If you take on a small task, it allows that person to get to work sooner. It will be appreciated.

Taking on other small tasks that show your willingness to pitch in will advance you into better jobs faster. One afternoon I asked a new employee to deliver some tapes to a client. Her response was, "Well, I don't want to do that right now. The traffic's really heavy." That was the wrong answer. My response was, "The client needs the tapes now, and it's either you or me . . . so you'd better get going." Her remark had demonstrated an unwillingness to do what was needed. To her credit, she never did that again and became a great worker. Other things you can do that will pay off are:

- Know the area where you live and work, and be able to drive around and find places on your own. If that means studying a city map at night, do it.
- Be more than punctual. Be early.
- If you work in an office environment, learn the ins and outs of fax machines, computers and photocopiers. Be able and willing to do the small fixes that are often necessary.
- Don't be surprised by overtime and weekend work. Both are common and expected. An average work week is sixty hours.

# 13. BECOME AN EXPERT AT LIBRARY AND INTERNET RESEARCH

Some library reference works are gold mines. Many media/communications fields have yearbooks. One is the *Broadcasting & Cable Yearbook*. This work starts with a preface that provides a concise description of major developments and trends in the field. The book is divided into specialties; within these you will find lists of organizations for radio, TV and cable. Also you will find sections on government agencies and ownership; equipment suppliers and services; programming suppliers; associations, education and awards; and books, periodicals and videos. You will also find a trade show week data book, *Ulrich's International Periodicals Directory Database*, published by R. R. Bowker, and *Bowker's Complete Video Directory*. This reference work also has a "Yellow Pages," section, providing addresses, phone numbers and key names within each organization. The *Yearbook* is valuable because of its comprehensive and specific information.

Almanacs are also a valuable resource, but for different reasons. One almanac to take note of is the latest *Information Please Almanac: The Ultimate Browser's Reference.* Look in the table of contents and index for topics in your specialty. For example, under the heading "Media" you will find lists of the leading magazines in the United States and Canada, the major U.S. daily newspapers and their circulations, addresses for the television networks, book awards and film revenues.

The Internet is becoming the resource of resources. Even if you don't have your own computer, most college students can gain access to the Internet at the on-campus computer lab. Many dorm computers now provide access as well. The Internet has several important uses for those preparing for the job market. First, it is an incredible research tool. You can find information about almost anything—the industries, the organizations and sometimes even the people you want to know about. Many jobs are listed on the Internet—many thousands of them. Second, you can promote yourself by putting your resumé in a virtual job bank. In fact, putting resumés and cover letters on the Internet is becoming a common method of launching a job search. Why not? It makes it easier for people, worldwide, to find you.

You will need full Internet access to make job searches. Before you begin, make a list of the specific job categories you are looking for. You will not get far unless you know the names of jobs, such as *copy writer, video producer* and so on. It's a learn-as-you-go process, and it is essential that you learn the proper keywords to use for searching. Most job banks will help you with this. Some search engines will require you to enter such information as job title, location, discipline (marketing, public relations) and salary range or to search by date of posting, so be ready to follow directions carefully. You will find that some search engines are easy to use, whereas others make the task more difficult than it's worth. There are job banks that list jobs for all fields, and there are job banks that are specific to the media and communications world.

However, doing an Internet job search is not as clear-cut as you would think. Many sites link you to other sites; for example, the jobs listed by *Advertising Age* link to another site called Monster Board. There are so many Web addresses that a good way to search is to get a small group of people together, divide the addresses among several people and have each person search ten addresses, taking careful notes or printing homepages with addresses and tables of contents. The record-keeping is important. Many people do not keep track of their searches and have no record of the useful information they have found. Internet searches may seem time-consuming, but they are not nearly as time-consuming as methods that preceded the Internet.

Some Internet sites tell about internships or reference works on subjects such as improving job interview skills. Others allow you to post your resumé—just follow the directions, which can differ for each job site. When doing this, remember to save your resumé as a plain-text file. This will eliminate any bold and italic type but will help ensure that your resumé is correctly formatted when it's posted.

I know several people who found their present jobs via the Internet. In fact, 10–15 percent of jobs are now filled through Internet postings. Others tell me that while they didn't find a job through the Internet, they were able to get four or five leads from online sources, some of which led to interviews. Once you get on the "short list" of those being considered for a particular job, you may be asked to answer questions via e-mail as a pre-interview technique.

In addition to the following lists of Internet job sites, you can consult any identifying organizations that would logically list jobs: for example, professional organizations such as the National Association of Broadcasters <http://www.nab.org>, industry trade publications such as *Advertising Age* <http://www.adage.com> and specific companies such as CBS <http://www.cbs.com>. NBC has a very interesting News Associates Program in which the network hires competent college graduates and moves them through several opportunities over a 10-month period. It's described in detail by following the links through job opportunities at <http://www.nbc.com>. Often you will see opportunities to get involved in Usenet, a collection of discussion groups called newsgroups. Newsgroups are organized by content areas. Jobs is one of the areas. By getting involved in newsgroups, you can ask questions and learn from others who are willing to trade tips. JOBTRAK <http://www.jobtrak.com> has a discussion group called JOBTRAK Career Forums that can be accessed through its homepage. You can post questions or get advice on "Careers in Entertainment and Communications" and the like. A typical address is <news:alt.jobs> for jobs in Atlanta or <news:tx.jobs> for opportunities in Texas. Many more such newsgroups can be easily accessed through Web portal sites and search engine career centers at Excite, Lycos, Netscape and Yahoo! via links on their homepages.

Another technique is to search by state, city or regional Web site. This is an excellent strategy; often you know what region of the country you want to live in even if you aren't sure what kind of job you want. Listed here are fourteen state Web site addresses; many of these sites have links to other regional or city job banks. You can easily find other state job banks through a Web search or a phone call to a state government office.

### State Job Banks

| | |
|---|---|
| Alabama | http://www.dir.state.al.us/esatl.jobs |
| Alaska | http://www.labor.state.ak.us |
| California | http://www.caljobs.ca.gov/ |
| Florida | http://www.state.fl.us/dles/Services/lfaj.htm |
| Georgia | http://www.dol.state.ga.useshtml/eshtml02.htm |
| Illinois | http://ides.state.il.us/htmlemployer.htm |
| Iowa | http://www.state.ia.us/government/wd |
| Maryland | http://www.careernet.state.md.us |
| Massachusetts | http://www.masscareers.state.ma.us |
| New York | http://www.labor.state.ny.us |
| Ohio | http://www.state.oh.us/obes |
| South Carolina | http://www.state.sc.us/jobs |
| Utah | http://www.state.ut.us/htmlemployment.htm |
| Wisconsin | http://www.dwd.state.wi.us/jobnet |

Following are lists of general and specific job banks, which are good places to start a job search, and of other career-related sites. I have placed an asterisk next to some of the larger job-bank sites. If these larger sites are not productive, try some of the smaller ones like <http://www.journalism.com> or <http://www.mediabistro.com>.

### General Job Banks

| | |
|---|---|
| American Jobs | http://www.AmericanJobs.com |
| *America's Job Bank | http://www.ajb.dni.us |
| Best Jobs | http://www.bestjobsusa.com |
| Broadcast Employment | http://www.tvjobs.com |
| *CareerBuilder Network | http://www.careerbuilder.com |
| Career Magazine | http://www.careermag.com |
| *CareerMosaic | http://www.careermosaic.com |
| CareerPath | http://www.careerpath.com |
| *College Grad Job Hunter | http://www.collegegrad.com |

| | |
|---|---|
| *Federal Jobs | http://www.fedworld.gov/jobs/ jobsearch.html |
| Fortune Magazine | http://www.fortune.com/careers |
| HeadHunter | http://www.headhunter.net |
| High-Tech Jobs | http://dice.com |
| HotJobs | http://www.hotjobs.com |
| JobBank USA | http://www.jobbankusa.com |
| JobHunt | http://www.job-hunt.org |
| JobTrak | http://www.jobtrak.com |
| Manpower | http://www.manpower.com |
| Marketing Jobs | http://www.marketingjobs.com |
| *Monster Board | http://www.monster.com |
| *National Association of Broadcasters | http://www.nab.org |
| *National Association of Colleges & Employers | http://www.jobweb.org |
| National Association of Television Program Executives | http://natpe.org |
| NationJob Network | http://www.nationjob.com |
| Recruiters Online Network | http://www.ipa.com |
| *Wall Street Journal | http://www.careers.wsj.com |
| Writing Jobs | http://www.writerswrite.com/jobs |
| Yahoo! Careers | http://careers.yahoo.com |

**Specific Job Banks**

| | |
|---|---|
| Advertising Sales Jobs | http://www.mediastaffingnetwork.com |
| AM/FM Radio Jobs | http://www.amfmradio.net |
| Asia Pacific Broadcasting Classifieds | http://www.apb-news.com |
| Asian American Journalists Association | http://www.aaja.org |
| Black Broadcasters Alliance | http://www.thebba.org |
| Broadcast News Talent | http://www.tvspy.com/jobs.htm |
| California Chicano News Media Association | http://www.ccnma.org |
| Entry-Level Jobs | http://www.mediabistro.com |
| Film, TV and Commercials Jobs | http://www.employnow.com |
| Investigative Reporters and Editors | http://www.ire.org/jobs |

Jobs for TV Professionals, Producers,
Promotions, Writers and Others    http://www.tvrundown.com/
resource/html
Journalism Jobs    http://www.journalismjobs.com
Specialized Postings    http://www.telecomcareers.net
Startups and Entrepreneurs    http://www.firsttuesday.com

**Other Career Resources**

Career-Planning Tips    http://www.jobhuntersbible.com
The Writing Center    http://www.rpi.edu/dept/llc/
writecenter/web/text/
coverltr.html
Business Job Finder    http://www.cob.ohio-state.edu/
dept/fin/osujobs.htm
The Pavement    http://www.thepavement.com

## 14. PROMOTE YOURSELF WITHOUT BEING OBNOXIOUS

This could easily be misinterpreted, but don't expect professors, bosses or other important people to automatically know what your competencies and life goals are (even if you have told them). If you are working on a class project, for example, it's to your benefit to keep track of your contributions, the hours you've spent and what you have learned. Write these things down. Although you hope it won't happen, while working on a group project you may need these records to defend yourself. Or you may need to explain to a professor why you have spent ten extra hours on the project. This could be considered self-promotion or just informing a person who evaluates you about your zeal in doing a good job. If done correctly and not too frequently, it will help you.

The same applies in the workplace: Making sure that your efforts are known is important. You can do this verbally, with a memo or by e-mail. Written records are especially important since they can be used during a performance evaluation, which most organizations conduct annually.

## 15. LEARN TO SPEAK AND WRITE A FOREIGN LANGUAGE

Computer-related fields have been mentioned as possible minors. Today one could also argue for making a foreign language a minor concentration in college, so that upon graduation you could speak and write a foreign language fluently. As I am writing this guidebook, I know of a local high-tech company that is advertising for technical writers. The company wants people with good writing skills in English and Spanish to write product descriptions for their catalog. Technical writers are in demand, but bilingual technical writers face very little competition. There is good money to be made, higher job security and greater mobility by knowing a second language.

Another opportunity a second language offers is travel. The world becomes your potential job market. That's an exciting possibility. With the uncertainty that communications/media professionals face, developing fluency in a second language is one of the best things you can do to enhance your career.

# TAKE ACTION

## 16. JOIN A PROFESSIONAL ORGANIZATION

Professional organizations exist for many reasons—to promote a specialization such as photography, marketing, or video games, and to provide services such as conferences, seminars, awards ceremonies and networking. Many organizations publish directories, newsletters and magazines. They hold annual meetings and assist local chapters, which usually meet monthly. All communications and media industries have at least one professional organization, and these groups are extremely valuable for both new and seasoned members. Many organizations have college chapters that are inexpensive to join and are advised by a professor. By the time you are a junior in college, it is advisable to be a member of at least the college chapter, attending the monthly meetings and taking part in any activities the group sponsors. Often, college chapters invite professionals from the community to speak at one of their meetings—a perfect time to learn more about the professional activities in your community, and a wonderful networking opportunity. Make it a goal to introduce yourself to these speakers, to make an impression on them, to see if you can get an invitation to visit their business, to get a business card. Even better, if you know of a research group or similar resource on campus that might help this speaker in his or her business, don't hesitate to tell the speaker about it and follow up if you can. Being helpful to someone makes it likely that you will be remembered.

The monthly meetings of many local off-campus professional chapters are held at a different business location each month. You can learn a lot by attending these meetings and seeing businesses firsthand. Employees of the business host the meeting, so you are often given personal tours in which the business activities are explained, meet a variety of employees and view the facilities. I found that many businesses are larger and more diversified than I had thought.

You have to realize that it is very difficult to get inside certain companies. By attending a professional organizational meeting, you are going as an honored guest; you may learn things you would not otherwise be told because you are part of a gathering of like-minded professionals. Not all professional chapters allow college-student members to attend meetings on a regular basis, but you should inquire.

While attending a meeting, you will be rubbing shoulders with professionals from various parts of your community and from different sections of the business. It probably would take weeks, even months, to drive around and meet all these people—even if you had the time to do so. So, when you get to attend a meeting such as this, treat it as a chance of a lifetime. After the meeting, make note of the people you met. Write down in your notebook any interesting things you learned that will help you reestablish a relationship with these people later, when you are ready for job hunting. If anyone at the meeting gives you advice or is especially helpful, write a thank-you note immediately. Remember that one of the most important things you can do to prepare yourself for life after college is to develop relationships with key people.

If you can't find a local professional organization in your specialty, or if you want more information about any of the organizations listed here, look in the reference section of your library for the *Encyclopedia of Organizations*. This reference work lists organizations under categories such as advertising, broadcasting and so on. Or conduct an Internet search by typing in the name of the organization as your keyword. It is also worthwhile to call the organization and ask about its activities, membership dues and publications. If while speaking with a representative you find that the organization doesn't seem appropriate for you, ask what other organizations might be better suited to your specialty. Here are some important professional organizations (and their phone numbers):

**Professional Organizations**

| | |
|---|---|
| Academy of Motion Picture Arts and Sciences | 310–247–3000 |
| Academy of Television Arts and Sciences (ATAS) | 818–754–2800 |

| | |
|---|---|
| Advertising Club of New York | 212–533–8080 |
| Advertising Production Club of New York | 212–983–6042 |
| Alliance for Health Care Strategy and Marketing | 312–704–9700 |
| American Advertising Federation (AAF) | 202–898–0089 |
| American Center for Design | 312–787–2018 |
| American Film Marketing Association (AFMA) | 310–446–1000 |
| American Institute of Graphic Arts | 212–807–1990 |
| American Marketing Association | 312–542–9000 |
| American News Women's Club | 202–332–6770 |
| American Society of Journalists and Authors | 212–997–0947 |
| American Society of Magazine Editors | 212–872–3700 |
| American Sportscasters Association (ASA) | 212–227–8080 |
| American Women in Radio and Television (AWRT) | 703–506–3290 |
| Asian American Journalists Association | 415–346–2051 |
| Associated Press Broadcasters | 202–736–1100 |
| Association for Women in Sports Media | 817–390–7409 |
| Association of Visual Communicators (AVC) | 619–461–1600 |
| Bank Marketing Association | 202–663–5268 |
| Black Women in Publishing | 212–772–5951 |
| Broadcast Designers' Association International | 310–712–0040 |
| Cable and Telecommunications: A Marketing Society | 703–549–4200 |
| Copywriters Council of America | 516–924–8555 |
| Creative Musicians Coalition | 309–685–4843 |
| | 800–882–4262 |
| Digital Printing and Imaging Association | 703–385–1339 |
| Direct Marketing Association | 212–768–7277 |
| Graphic Artists Guild Foundation | 212–791–3400 |
| Graphic Arts Technical Foundation | 412–741–6860 |
| Graphic Communications Association | 703–519–8160 |
| Hollywood Radio and Television Society | 818–789–1182 |
| International Advertising Association | 212–557–1133 |
| International Animated Film Society, ASIA-Hollywood | 818–842–8330 |
| International Association of Business Communicators (ABC) | 415–433–3400 |
| International Documentary Association (IDA) | 310–284–8422 |
| International Food, Wine & Travel Writers Association | 562–433–5969 |
| International Interactive Communications Society | 510–608–5930 |
| International Public Relations Association | 561–416–5870 |
| International Radio and Television Society Foundation | 212–867–6650 |
| International Television and Video Association | 214–869–1112 |

| | |
|---|---|
| International Women's Writing Guild (IWW) | 212–737–7536 |
| Internet Society | 703–648–9888 |
| | 800–468–9507 |
| Magazine Publishers of America (MPA) | 212–872–3700 |
| National Academy of Television Arts and Sciences | 212–586–8424 |
| National Association of Broadcasters (NAB) | 202–429–5300 |
| National Association of College Broadcasters | 401–863–2225 |
| National Association of Media Women | 404–827–1718 |
| National Association of Minority Media Executives | 888–968–7658 |
| National Association of Radio Talk Show Hosts | 617–437–9757 |
| National Association of Television Programming Executives (NATPE) | 310–453–4440 |
| National Cable Television Association (NCTA) | 202–775–3550 |
| New Media Society | 703–243–0145 |
| New York New Media Association (NYNMA) | 212–785–7898 |
| Public Relations Society of America (PRSA) | 212–995–2230 |
| Publishers Marketing Association | 310–372–2732 |
| Radio Advertising Bureau | 212–681–7200 |
| | 800–232–3131 |
| Radio-Television Correspondents Association (RTCA) | 202–224–6421 |
| Retail Advertising and Marketing Association | 312–251–7262 |
| Romance Writers of America | 281–440–6885 |
| Society of Publication Designers | 212–983–8585 |
| Video Software Dealers Association | 818–385–1500 |
| Women in Film (WIF) | 213–463–6040 |

# 17. FIND INTERNSHIPS AND BE A COMPETENT INTERN

It's hard to find a textbook, career guide, even a pamphlet that doesn't recommend internships to students. That's because internships provide low-risk experiences. You're there to learn; everyone knows that, so you can participate in many different activities as an assistant—an ideal learning situation. Because internships are so important, they require special planning on your part.

First, an internship will be valuable only if the organization is willing to provide you with a rounded experience. Large companies with established internship programs are usually adept at providing worthwhile activities. Beware of small companies, however, unless they have a steady workload or a large project you can work on. If they do, you might have a very productive internship because small companies may need you to perform several different jobs. In some cases, interns get to produce real communications, sit in on real meetings and have the opportunity to make decisions. In other cases, however, interns are given meaningless tasks or sit at a desk reading the newspaper for a good portion of each day. An internship looks good on a resumé, but you want more than that. You want and need an experience that will help you learn specific skills and allow you to observe a wide range of activities. Even better, internships can lead to jobs. What better way for a company to get to know a potential employee than by having an intern in the office for three months? The same is true for the intern. Internships provide a firsthand learning experience, one that cannot come from a textbook.

Finding a good internship is like looking for an apartment. You don't know much unless you compare one opportunity with another. Once you investigate several internships, you'll be able to add up the advantages and disadvantages of each. College placement officers or student advisors can explain the internship process at your institution. Normally, companies are listed with the college placement office, which matches interns to the companies. But many internships are not advertised. Talk with your advisor or major professors about your interests. Some professors may have recently changed careers, coming from a communications business to a university to teach; others consult or perform part-time communications work; many attend professional meetings. These professors know which businesses in your community provide internships and may be able to put you in touch with key people. If you connect with a company that is interested in providing an internship but is not registered with your college, you may be able to ensure that the organization does get properly listed by coordinating and following up on the process. This is good experience in itself. Though time-consuming, the effort is worthwhile because an internship can be one of your most valuable and productive college experiences. And there's no pressure because you are not asking for a job.

An excellent way to evaluate the value of particular internships is to talk with students presently working as interns or, better yet, to visit them at work. Find out the good, the bad and the ugly. Nothing beats firsthand experience. You might learn things about parking (perhaps you'd have to pay $8 or more a day) and office conditions. You'll be able to make better judgments about the work, about whether you'd be comfortable with the people there and about whether you think they'd be comfortable with you. The comfort factor is a critical ingredient for a first internship. If you're not comfortable in the situation for any reason, or if you sense the employer is not comfortable with you, the internship is probably not going to work well for you. In fact, it could turn into a negative situation.

If you can't visit the place of business, ask an intern to tell you about the kind of work he or she performs there. Finally, if you don't know anyone at a particular business, make a phone call and see if you can schedule a time to visit. Don't accept an internship sight unseen. Just like apartment hunting, you don't have to take the first one you see. It's best to find three or four internship possibilities. Investigate each one, make visits and then decide. Good internships are competitive. You may not get the one you most want—which is a good reason to have backups. In addition, remember that everyone working in a communications business is extremely busy. Make sure you find out all you can ahead of time, without taking valuable time from a communicator's schedule.

How far in advance should you start working on finding an internship? That depends on many factors—whether you know what you want to do, whether you have the prerequisites completed and so on. But the earlier the better. If you're planning to get involved in an internship during your junior year, you should start investigating the possibilities in the fall of your sophomore year.

Many students are interested in particular internships in distant locations. One of my students in Pittsburgh spent a summer at Universal Studios in Florida. This took a great deal of coordination with her parents and with Universal. She applied one semester prior to her internship (which wasn't ideal timing), met the application deadlines, filed the appropriate forms (including required letters of recommendation) and made a special trip for an interview. While there, she looked into housing arrangements. At first she didn't think she would be accepted into the program, and once accepted, she was hesitant to take it because of the distance and the money involved. But she did finally decide to spend a summer at Universal. It turned out to be a highlight of her college career.

If you have a favorite magazine, television program, newspaper or film company, it's likely the company has an internship program. Long-distance internships take more research and more work to find out about and apply to, and they're often very competitive. If this idea strikes your fancy, start planning; it can be done. A high-profile or unique internship can give a competitive edge to your resumé. It shows that you think seriously about your career, and that you're willing to take risks and invest extra time and effort in your preparation. It also provides excellent conversation for a job interview.

One good resource for internships is *Internships: 50,000 On-the-Job Training Opportunities for Students and Adults,* which is published annually by Peterson's Guides, Inc., Princeton, NJ 08543. The phone number is 800–338–3282.

For the most current internship possibilities, it's hard to beat what the Internet offers. One Web site devoted entirely to internships is Rising Star Internships <http://www.rsinternships.com>. To find more information on internships, conduct a keyword search through a Web site like Yahoo! There you will find not only additional internship directories but also listings for specific internships listed by organization (such as NASA), by city or by region.

If you want your internship to go really well, be prepared to be a good listener and observer. You have the chance to observe the day-to-day environment, so observe everything. Here are some questions to keep in mind before you get "on-the-job."

When do people normally arrive at and leave work?
What's a typical daily or weekly workload? Does it normally involve
    evenings and weekends?
What about the quality of the work produced, and the criteria on
    which the work is judged? Evaluate both in your own mind.
How do people react to stress?
How is conflict handled?
How do people balance their work and outside-of-work pursuits?
How do people dress?
What are the attitudes toward women and minorities?

All of these questions will help you decipher corporate culture. It's different everywhere, and it's important to understand. Other things to keep in mind are:

**Be an appropriate participator.**   Let's say that you are an intern at an ad agency and you are invited to sit in on a brainstorming meeting. Before the meeting starts, people begin telling funny stories about work-related incidents. Should you tell one? No. You are not in a position to hold up the meeting or dominate attention. The joking and chatter often have meaning beyond the moment. Even if it's not on a conscious level, a good deal of positioning is being done through joking and storytelling. For example, someone might tell a story about a project that he worked on at a previous company and how it ran into serious problems, how he stayed up all night to meet the deadline, and how everyone loved the final result. These "saved-the-day" stories are typical and are enjoyed by others because they have had similar experiences. The *real* story is that these anecdotes establish the employee's competence, stamina and commitment to excellence. Let them do that. Your job is to listen, learn and enjoy.

However, if you're asked to research a topic, produce initial storyboards or write drafts, you should begin immediately. In most cases, asking questions as you go is fine. But if you are uncomfortable with an assigned task—because you haven't done it before (perhaps they think you have) or you don't know where to start—make that known immediately. Most communications work is produced on a tight schedule, and waiting only makes things worse. Professionals often forget what experience has brought them in accomplishing work quickly and productively. This means that an open and comfortable relationship is best for you, one in which you can express your concerns and ask questions.

Whenever you can, participate in outside-of-work activities. For example, if the company is planning its annual community day, when employees provide community services such as helping the elderly or painting houses, offer to take part. If you are invited to join others for lunch, arrange your schedule and finances so that it's possible for you to attend. People will get to know you in a different way; you will begin to see what you have in common with people who may be quite different from you. You may even meet someone who can be a mentor.

**Be as knowledgeable in your field as you can.**   Review key points and terminology from your textbooks so that you are prepared to do what's asked during the course of the internship. This is where your coursework and good study habits pay off.

**Do an attitude check.**   Be positive, and realize at all times that as an intern you are there to help the business. Do more than what's needed. Arrive earlier than expected. Stay late if you see you can help and your schedule permits.

## 18.  GET A PART-TIME JOB IN YOUR FIELD

If an internship can provide you with useful on-the-job experience, just think what a well-selected summer job in your field can do. Many internships are unpaid, so a summer job in your field can really pay off—in more ways than one.

Since many students don't declare a major until their sophomore year, you really have only two summers to explore jobs related to your field of study—the summer between your sophomore and junior years, and the one between your junior and senior years. To make these two summers pay off, start planning during your first year in college.

A lot of students stay with the kind of job they had in high school—counter person at a fast-food restaurant, lifeguard at a pool, waiter and so on. That's okay if you think a job is going to fall in your lap after graduation, but by now you know better. Again, attitude and motivation are the key factors. It's going to take an investigative, hard-charging approach to find something that can help you develop a career rather than just earn money for the summer.

Some people live in large cities where there are plenty of opportunities. If you do, use that to your advantage. But if you live in a small town or rural area where there are far fewer opportunities, you will have to look high and low to find something worthwhile. If you can't find something suitable, consider living for a summer with a relative or friend in a city where opportunities abound. Again, these things take considerable effort. The planning will demand sacrifices, but you have to keep asking yourself how important that job after college is to you. The more you prepare, the better off you'll be.

## 19.  VOLUNTEER

Provide communications services on a volunteer basis for small or campus-related organizations. For example, write press releases for your sorority or soccer team, help out a TV station sponsoring a 10k run, offer to deliver things, help out in a crisis, do the behind-the-scenes work or do whatever else is necessary. If it's not directly communications work, that's okay. Volunteering will often bring you unexpected rewards, such as opportunities to meet professionals who might hire you someday.

## 20.  CALL AND VISIT

If you hear of a communications business or project that sounds interesting, try to find a way to visit and see what's going on. Make a cold call and explain your interest. "Would it be possible to visit?" Often the answer will be yes. If the answer is no, try different businesses. Many students are afraid to make cold calls, but you should realize that students have a special status. In a sense your status is neutral: You're nonthreatening because you are not yet looking for a job and because you are expressing a desire to learn. Most professionals, even the busy ones, will try to help a student because the professional can remember being in the same position. If one professional can't help you, ask if there is someone else who can. Remember, when you make a cold call, your job is to establish a relationship with the first person you talk to, so that if necessary you can be referred to someone else who can help you. Businesses are very specialized, and larger businesses may have a communications department whose job it is to assist people like yourself. Even in smaller businesses you may have to go through several referrals to find someone helpful. But make that your goal: Find someone who can help you. Don't expect it to be the first person on the other end of the line.

In addition, when making cold calls to organizations, be prepared to navigate the voice-mail system. In some cases that may mean just staying on the line or dialing zero. If cold-calling does not work out for you, try e-mailing the organization. Once you know one e-mail address you can often figure out others, and many people, even top-level executives, will respond to you faster by e-mail than by telephone. The main thing to remember is that communicating with professionals as a student is likely to yield positive results.

Another possibility is to go on class-sponsored field trips or tag along (with permission, of course) with a different class on its field trip. Set a goal to make a couple of visits during the school year and at least one over the summer. Take along your resumé. I have seen job offers made to students who have left their resumés at companies during field visits.

## 21. DEVELOP MENTORS

Become comfortable with people who are older and who are in prestigious or interesting positions, including professors, older students who are working and attending classes, graduate students, people you meet on your summer jobs or during field visits, people you meet when you attend a professional organization's meetings, parents of friends, neighbors and so on. Many students are afraid to become friendly with people who are in successful positions, but avoiding such people or failing to cultivate relationships with them is a mistake. Certain people enjoy helping a student learn about an industry or a particular opportunity. Show an interest in learning about an area; show an interest in improving your situation. If you show your motivation, people will be more likely to help you. Making connections is the first step. When you do establish relationships, don't forget to follow up. That means thanking individuals in writing, but it also means staying in touch. You can do this through occasional phone calls or e-mail. You can do more than thank people. Once you know of someone's interests, you may find newspaper or magazine articles that you feel are of interest to that individual—send them on with a note. Or you could simply keep someone informed of your progress.

To do any of this, you need good record-keeping—a file with names, addresses, phone numbers and e-mail addresses. Take notes on what you discussed; keep track of people's interests, children, hobbies. This doesn't mean being a snoop or being strange; it means being interested in people. Developing mentors takes a bit of self-analysis and guts. You need to know your own strengths and weaknesses; a mentor can help you improve in weak areas if you are willing to discuss such things. Mentors can refer you to other people or give you advice on how to handle a difficult situation. Mentors are important once you are in a job, too. Many work situations are difficult for new employees; often, personal and business paths can cross in odd directions—you may need advice that hinges on an ethical problem, for example. Sometimes it's even hard for veterans to know what to do. If you have someone you trust, you can talk and figure out a plan. This can be invaluable for those who want to progress steadily up the ladder to better jobs and better pay.

## 22. SEEK NEW OPPORTUNITIES

Take a look at yourself and your goals. What strengths do you have that will help you accomplish those goals? What are your main weaknesses that will prevent you from succeeding? I suggest you begin to think about how you can strengthen your weakest areas. It could be through selecting certain electives in your college coursework, or by looking for opportunities outside college. Talk to your department chair, professors, graduate assistants, fellow students or your college career or placement officer about what you're looking for. For example, you may want to improve your ability in working with certain computer programs; if coursework isn't appropriate, find special short-term sessions. These may be listed at computer stores or advertised in a local paper or business newsweekly. A tutor at the campus computer lab may be able to help you learn a few things about a particular computer program. You may be amazed at how a little informal tutoring can advance your skills. You just have to have a questioning mind and be persistent in seeking out these kinds of opportunities.

Another possibility is to take short courses over a break or summer vacation. Devote one week to learning something new. Professional organizations hold workshops in team building or public speaking, for example. There may be something offered in a one-day session or a few hours one evening; these sessions might open new areas of interest for you. Look in industry magazines for upcoming conferences, meetings and workshops, which in most fields are held year-round in various locations. You may have to travel and you may have to pay, but if the experience will teach a specific skill you feel you need to have, it will be worth it.

If you want to improve your interpersonal or group communications skills, consider joining an organization called Toastmasters or taking a Dale Carnegie course. Look for whatever is available and within your budget.

Highly recommended workshops in film, video, multimedia and other topics are conducted by the Maine Photographic Workshops of Rockport, Maine (phone 207–236–8581; Web site <http://www.MEWork shops.com>).

## 23. BECOME AWARE OF CORPORATE CULTURE

If you think that understanding corporate culture is a bit of a puzzle, you're not alone. It can take months or years to fully understand an organization's culture. You may find this to be true in your college department, your dorm, your family and your workplace. It's a puzzle because the rituals, stories and regulations that make up corporate culture are not written down, openly recognized or discussed, yet everyone in the organization seems to know what they are and when they are being violated. You can learn about corporate culture by being a good listener and observer. For example, attendance at holiday parties may be mandatory even though it seems that it is not. Overtime may be expected, particularly on the part of newly hired employees. Dress is a part of corporate culture. Corporate culture is not something to be afraid of, but it is something you need to be sensitive to. If you choose not to conform to it, you will be doing it by choice, not by accident.

# 24. ATTEND CAREER WORKSHOPS AND FAIRS

Both career workshops and career fairs are plentiful. Recruiters use them as a preferred method for identifying prospective employees because they get to meet the candidates face to face and conduct brief interviews. In many cases, workshops and fairs are held at the same time and location so that you can take advantage of both. Workshops cover topics such as preparing resumés and developing interview skills. Fairs bring together employers who set up kiosks and supply company representatives who can tell you about the types of jobs available. Normally, the people at these fairs are good and knowledgeable communicators. Career fairs may be general in focus (covering many different industries) or specialized. I've seen creative-career fairs, business-related fairs and computer/information-systems-related fairs. Cities sponsor career fairs, as do most colleges and community colleges.

Career fairs are extremely worthwhile to attend. You should start doing so long before you look for a real job. There is no other way a college student can know about the enormous number of companies doing business and the types of jobs they offer. It is truly mind-boggling. Career fairs are concentrated experiences where you can spend an hour and receive a lifetime of benefits. All you have to do is walk around and begin talking with people. If you're close to graduation, you can have one kind of conversation with a representative; if graduation is a few years off, you can have another kind. Let's say that you're a sophomore and not sure of what you want to do after college. You could learn general trivia—who is at the fair, who looks interesting and so on. Or you could strike up a few conversations and begin to learn what a certain company is like and the types of positions it offers. You might learn a specific fact that's really useful—for example, that a company is opening a new division next year in Florida and will be hiring about 200 employees. You might learn that a corporation seems very formal and therefore doesn't interest you. Even though a career fair may not be focused on internships or summer work, there's nothing stopping you from asking for and getting a contact to call. It's great when you can write or call someone and say, "So-and-so suggested I talk with you." Your chances of connecting with someone are much greater when you are referred.

If you run out of questions, ask about the types of people the company has hired recently and the kind of background and life experience the company is looking for in its employees. Ask also about the company's locations, benefits and so on. Your questioning is like an open book—

you just have to have a curious mind and a few questions ready. The rest will happen by itself. Look for news of upcoming career fairs in the college newspaper, city business newsweekly or local newspaper. Also check the Web pages of these print publications. Fairs are usually well advertised. If your college isn't having a career fair, check with colleges nearby. You could find out by calling the career office at another institution or by calling the mayor's office or Chamber of Commerce about fairs being sponsored by the city government.

When you attend a career fair, it's very important that you dress appropriately. Wear the same type of clothing you would wear to a job interview—that is, fairly conservative business attire.

## 25. GO TO BOOKSTORES

The value of a bookstore over a library is that in a bookstore you will find the latest releases. And when you're researching the internship or job market, you want the most current resources that you can find. If you go to several bookstores, you may find one that consistently has the best career section. You don't have to make special trips to most bookstores. There may be one near a movie theater or in a shopping mall where you often go. Begin stopping in bookstores on your way to somewhere else, but allow extra time if you can. You may find that you're staying longer than planned because you are finding so many references that interest you. Another advantage of bookstores these days is that many have great coffee bars. Normally, you can take books into these areas and leisurely browse through them before you buy. Don't forget to browse the magazine and newspaper sections of the larger bookstores, where you will likely find a very wide selection of publications, including some you may not be aware of. Many bookstores also provide an excellent selection of CD-ROM and multimedia titles, music areas and even Internet access. They've become wonderful resource/meeting/chatting places.

## 26. APPLY FOR GRANTS AVAILABLE
##    TO STUDENTS

Posted on your department or dorm bulletin board, you will occasionally find organizations advertising a grant for a student to develop and produce a communications product. This is a wonderful opportunity; it is probably something you would attempt in your junior or senior year. For example, the University Film and Video Association offers the Carole Fielding Student Grant (<http://raven.ubalt.edu/staff/simon/ufvagrants.html>)

which awards $4,000 for film, video or multimedia production and up to $1,000 for research. This project requires a proposal, but completing the application requirements (such as purpose statement, audience, schedule and budget) is terrific experience. If you were to receive such a grant and complete a high-quality project, it would be extremely helpful—both to your resumé and as a learning experience. The Broadcast Education Association (<http://www.bea.org>) offers several scholarships for communications and media students: the BEA Two-Year Community College Award (two scholarships of $1,500 each), the Andrew M. Economos Scholarship ($5,000), the Shane Media Scholarship ($3,000), the Abe Voron Scholarship ($5,000) and several others. For details visit the BEA Web site.

## 27. TAKE AN INDEPENDENT STUDY

If there is a project you would like to complete or if you have a specific area of interest but no course is offered in that area, consider taking an independent or directed study. By doing so, you could work with one professor and pursue your specialty. Independent study is a good way to work with a professor whose professional expertise you would like to learn and draw from.

## 28. KEEP A PORTFOLIO OF YOUR WORK

Keep in a safe place all of your best papers, scripts, photographs, press kits, research projects, magazine and newspaper articles, videos, multimedia work, graphic design projects and whatever else represents your talents and hard work. Assume that you will be asked to show some of these items to prospective employers. Organize and edit this material so that the best of your portfolio can be carried and shown easily and quickly. If you can, make at least two copies of your portfolio so that you can leave one copy with an employer if necessary.

# DEVELOP AN ATTITUDE FOR SUCCESS

## 29. ASK YOURSELF, "AM I A SEXIST, A RACIST OR A SNOB?"

Often, we don't recognize our own attitudes and biases. If you know you have trouble in this area, do something positive to correct it. Everyone deserves an equal amount of respect and an equal chance to succeed. I believe those who recognize this and behave accordingly will excel.

## 30. DEVELOP ATTITUDE AND PASSION

These personal attributes matter more to me when I'm hiring someone than most anything else. If a person is competent and knowledgeable, he or she certainly has the foundation required for good work. But a lack of proper attitude and passion infiltrates all phases of a person's life like a disease. What good are intelligence and skill if they are not applied or are applied without the diligence, stamina and sense of excitement needed in the workplace? I would rather teach someone with a strong work ethic the ins and outs of a job, because once that person knows what to do, it will be done well. A person who cares is consistently reliable. Attitude and passion don't come easily. If going to college is your work, then attitude and passion for what you do will bring you good grades and positive recommendations when you graduate. These attributes mean that you maintain high standards even under duress, that you never give up and that you find a way to solve problems. If you can develop these attributes in college, you will be a leader and well prepared for the world of work. Work demands these qualities daily.

## 31. EMPHASIZE TRUSTWORTHINESS AND POSITIVE ATTITUDES

Being trustworthy in all aspects of your life is necessary for you to be successful. To others, trustworthiness means that they can count on you no matter what the circumstances.

Being positive seems to be difficult for many people, so if you can consistently present a reasonably positive attitude, you will stand out. I say *reasonably* because an artificially overly positive attitude is not what I mean. Negative attitudes abound everywhere, and they're a waste of time and energy. However, finding ways to maintain a positive attitude through difficult times takes heroic effort. I suggest you read at least one of Stephen J. Covey's books, such as *The Seven Habits of Highly Effective People, Principle-Centered Leadership* or *First Things First: To Live, to Love, to Learn, to Leave a Legacy*. These books discuss positive attitudes, trustworthiness and much more. You can find them in most libraries and bookstores.

## 32. DON'T BURN YOUR BRIDGES

It's an old saying but you see the value of it all the time. Something goes wrong for you on the job—something as simple as an argument over the direction of a project—and you see how easy it is to lash out at people who you feel are being unfair to you. Employees become emotionally involved in their work and resent those who interfere. Tempers flare and relationships can be damaged. Or it could be more serious and result in your movement to a new section of the company, your failure to get a promotion or even a layoff. Because the media industry is not that big, you can expect to keep running into the same people. It's best to patch up differences and leave a company on good terms. Badmouthing your former bosses and colleagues may come back to haunt you.

## 33. WRITE YOUR IDEAL RESUMÉ

As early in your college career as possible, write a one- to two-page resumé that includes the grade point average, internships, work experiences, volunteer and special activities, professional memberships, awards and anything else you would like to earn or take part in during your college years. Dream a little. Give yourself something to work toward. For example, jotting down some specific summer work experiences on paper will make it easier for you to focus on and achieve that goal. The same is true for any other experience or opportunity you aspire to. You will almost always achieve more when you work toward clearly defined goals.

# 4

# QUESTIONS AND ANSWERS

Once you get close to job-hunting time, you'll begin asking very specific questions. This chapter answers some common questions.

**1. Do some jobs pay more?** The simple answer is that it doesn't matter. The job you get must fit you, and you must be ready to perform. Starting pay is not high in the communications/media industries no matter where you go, ranging from $20,000 to $35,000 yearly. You will find that salaries are higher in larger cities. For all media and communications work that I know of, working on projects that are distributed nationally involves more prestige and pays better than working on regional or local projects. Regional work usually pays better than local work. Some of the differences in pay are shocking. For example, the pay for directing a local television commercial is likely to be based on a rate of $500–$1,000 per day; for directing a high-end regional commercial, $3,000–$7,000 per day; and for directing a prestigious national commercial, $10,000–$20,000 or more per day. A staff director of local television news might be paid an annual salary of $35,000–$50,000; a director of national soap operas often makes $2,000 or more per episode.

**2. Do some jobs have more potential for advancement?** Jobs related to creative, sales and management functions generally have the most potential for advancement. Jobs related to technical functions—or what some people consider craft/skill functions (camera person, audio person)—do not normally put you in the fast lane to higher management positions. Advancement in a skill area usually comes by way of working on bigger, more prestigious projects, for which the pay is higher. However, many of these jobs have the protection provided by union membership.

**3. Can I transfer from one field of communications to another?** It's not easy to move from one media/communications industry to another. Some people manage to do so, but it takes a concerted effort. Also difficult is a move from a creative job to a sales job, for example. Jobs are usually seen as creative, technical, sales *or* administrative. Unless a person demonstrates exceptional talent, there is resistance to moving someone from one category to another.

**4. Should I work freelance rather than full-time?** Freelance employment, where people are paid a day rate for their work, is a big part of communications and media fields. Writers, graphic artists, camera and sound people and so on are often hired on a freelance basis. For most young people right out of school, however, freelance work is not a very good idea. Such work is intriguing because day rates seem high; sometimes overtime is paid and travel is involved. But there are no guarantees with this kind of work, and often no benefits such as health care, retirement, withholding of federal and state taxes or matching of Social Security tax. You can spend a lot of time looking for work, never knowing when you will be hired. You can also wait 60 to 90 days to be paid. Freelance work may serve as a temporary solution while you are looking for a full-time job, but be sure that such jobs don't stop you from looking. If the freelance opportunity exposes you to full-time openings, then it's an ideal situation, getting you in the door without your having to write a formal application letter.

With that being said, even if you work on-staff in a communications organization, you will be working with freelancers. Media and communications work is usually thought of in terms of projects (programs, issues, CDs etc.) so it often takes a burst of energy to accomplish a project, then (if you're lucky) there is a break, followed by another burst of energy to accomplish the next project. The work is often accomplished by one communications organization that is responsible for the overall project. But sections of the project may be subcontracted to other organizations or individuals who specialize in writing, graphics, production and other areas. Some people work almost full-time on a freelance basis for a single organization, particularly in the advertising and public relations industries. Although such an arrangement is appealing, it is also risky. For example, if a problem arises with the freelancer's work, the firm could easily stop hiring the freelancer or delay payments. If the firm itself has a problem, it will have no more work to subcontract—and such unexpected developments can happen overnight with the loss of a large contract.

# 5

# JOB DIRECTORY

Jobs in the media and communications fields can be divided into five general categories: Management, Sales, Creative Services, Technical Areas, and New Media/Multimedia. However, these five categories cover many different specialties. And they vary in the range of responsibilities between large and small companies. Managers in small companies are much more likely to delve into creative work, go out on sales calls or fix equipment—all depending on their skills and what needs to be done. Larger firms employ specialists in order to maintain a more strict division of labor. And wherever there are labor unions, you will find job responsibilities well defined.

Whether you choose to work for a large or small company is an important consideration. Small companies may provide you with a greater variety of tasks and, therefore, a wider range of work experience. Large companies may provide you with experience on larger, more prestigious projects. Small companies are likely to have a more informal atmosphere, whereas large companies may provide better salaries and benefits. There are advantages and disadvantages to each, but you should be aware of the differences so you can choose the environment you find most comfortable. Internships and part-time work can help you understand the differences between the working conditions and expectations of large and small companies.

Following is a brief description of the types of job titles or positions that fall within each of the five general job categories.

**Management** includes Department Heads, Vice Presidents, Presidents, Chief Executive Officers and Chief Financial Officers. Some department heads are called *directors* or *chiefs*, such as News Director or Editor in Chief. These jobs obviously require experience and demonstrated competence, since the health of the organization is directly related to the vision and leadership of its top management. Whereas job titles such as *vice president* or *director* may seem to exclude creative or technical work, managers in small companies are much more likely to keep their hands in a wider variety of activities. Since media and communications work is centered on teamwork and on completing projects (such as advertising campaigns, television programs, magazine issues and radio shows), often doing so on tight deadlines, managers must be adept at supervising small groups and solving problems quickly. Management styles that allow for flexibility and creativity yet still provide the leadership to drive projects forward are typical of successful media managers.

**Sales** positions are often linked with marketing and promotions, but they are in fact three different specialties. *Marketing* focuses on analyzing target audiences and positioning product; *sales* is based on direct interaction with clients and on closing deals; *promotions* work draws attention to an organization or product by getting involved in special events, contests, giveaways and the like. Radio stations are heavily involved in promotional projects.

**Creative Services** involve production of any print, electronic or computer communication. *Programming, production* and *editorial* are names of departments using creative employees such as writers, producers, animators and designers. Creative people often work on teams with account managers so that the elements of a project can move ahead on schedule, on budget and in an orderly manner. Those professionals who work in corporate communications and write speeches or produce videos are usually considered to be part of Creative Services.

**Technical Areas** maintain equipment and coordinate the proper technologies with projects so that communications work can be planned, produced, distributed and evaluated. Video-editing equipment may have to be reconfigured or relocated from project to project. Satellite time must be scheduled. Computers may have to be installed and set up with software and so on. Technology is particularly important to the production and distribution of communications, but it is involved in all phases of the business. This area is becoming more important—jobs are on the increase.

**New Media/Multimedia** jobs are growing rapidly in number. These jobs usually require working with computer technology. New media jobs can exist within any organization. Corporations, television networks, universities, radio stations and newspapers employ individuals who create interactive presentations, communications stored on CD-ROMS or material for a Web page. These positions often require both creative skills and knowledge of complex software programs. Thus, they fall under neither the creative nor the technical areas described earlier.

Following you will find brief descriptions of typical jobs in eight media/communications business areas. Obviously, there are many more positions than can be covered here, but this list will give you an idea of the types of jobs available and the job responsibilities that go with the titles. You will find similar positions in the other communications industries not mentioned. More detailed information can be found in the references listed in the Additional Resources section at the back of this book.

## ADVERTISING

*Account Executive.*    Oversees accounts with agency clients so that advertising campaigns are both creatively and efficiently managed. The account executive can be seen as a liaison between client and agency who tries to keep both the client and the agency happy. It is a high-visibility, challenging job, and is often well paid.

*Senior Broadcast Producer.*    Coordinates activities with outside production firms that produce commercials and other creative work. This person identifies various directors who shoot/direct commercials, collects bid packets from directors and production houses that are vying to work on a campaign, sets up call times and production details with directors contracted by an agency and oversees the production of the commercial.

*Media Buyer.*    Buys the time and space for advertising and negotiates pricing with various media. This is a unique job, unlike any other in the agency. The person who has this job must be good at "cutting deals."

*Production Manager.*    Coordinates and schedules the activities with outside production houses contracted by the agency, such as studio time and audio-production facilities for voice-overs. The person who has this job must be able to juggle many projects at once and coordinate with both outside companies and in-house agency people to make sure the work is properly completed. The production manager must understand all phases of advertising production.

*Art Director.*    Oversees design of graphics, animation, signage, shelf-cards, the "look" of television commercials and so on. This person attends still-photo shoots and film or video production for commercials. He or she works closely with the creative people hired by an agency so that the agency achieves the content and creative goals planned in the campaign.

*Copy Writer.* Writes radio, television or print advertising. Scripts are submitted for approval to clients, and changes are common. Rewriting is a big part of the job. Creativity, ability to write quickly and knowledge of script-writing software are prerequisites for this job.

*Artist/Designer.* Draws or creates computer graphics, including advertising art, animatics (first-draft storyboards for commercials), production storyboards, new business presentation art, print layouts and Web pages.

*Assistant Positions.* Many departments have jobs with the word *assistant* in the title and in most cases these jobs are beginning-level positions. The job responsibilities depend on the experience and ability of the individual. These jobs provide ample opportunity for beginners to learn many aspects of the advertising business. Typical assistant positions are media assistant, production assistant, advertising assistant, marketing assistant and assistant copy writer.

*Note:* Public relations agencies have a structure similar to that of advertising agencies, and many of the jobs have similar titles. One exception is the job of media buyer, a position not normally found in a public relations agency.

# INSTITUTIONAL COMMUNICATIONS AND TRAINING (CORPORATE, GOVERNMENT, NONPROFITS)

*Director of Communications.* Oversees the many facets of corporate communications, which usually involves directing a staff that creates and distributes print, electronic and computer communications. These jobs may cross into some facets of public relations, advertising and promotion. This person oversees hiring and coordinating work with freelance artists, designers, photographers, videographers, writers and various printing and production companies.

*Director of Media Relations.* Handles inquiries from newspaper, magazine, television/cable, radio and Web personnel. This person promotes stories, events, products or services to the media. He or she must often interface with the media during a crisis or negative situation.

*Desktop Publishing Specialist.* Combines text, visuals and design elements to create brochures and a wide variety of other documents for internal and external use of the company.

*Writer.*   Writes a wide variety of communications—annual reports, press releases, press kits, brochures, in-house newsletters, videos, multimedia, promotional and sales materials, trade show and meeting materials, new business pitches, responses to customers, technical documents and training materials.

*Speech Writer.*   Researches and writes speeches for top-level management.

*Artist.*   Creates a variety of art, usually on computer, for use in all communications. Artists may be involved in a wide variety of the work noted for writers, including videos, newsletters, technical communications and so on. They may also design trade-show kiosks and sales areas.

*Camera Operator/Videographer.*   Records scenes on videotape or film. The individual in this position may also be responsible for directing talent, carrying equipment, interacting with clients and overseeing lighting.

*Technical Engineer.*   Participates in the selection, installation and maintenance of audio, video, computer and transmission equipment and facilities.

*Training and Development Manager.*   Supervises the creation, delivery and assessment of training programs. Often these programs use a variety of media delivered through computers and videotape.

*Training Specialist.*   Plans, organizes, directs and delivers a wide range of training programs. For example, training specialists might conduct orientation sessions or programs on health benefits and retirement programs. Usually they assess the need for training, develop the materials and participate in the training sessions.

*Video/Multimedia Editor.*   Edits various visual communications. This person is usually familiar with sophisticated computer linear and non-linear videotape and multimedia-editing equipment.

## MAGAZINE PUBLISHING

*Publisher.*   Supervises all activities of the magazine from production to circulation. The publisher sets the editorial policy and oversees financial operations.

*Managing Editor.*   Oversees the editorial and production departments to maintain quality and meet deadlines.

*Staff Writer.*   Writes features or columns, usually in a particular content area—politics, gardening, or the computer industry, for example.

*Copy Editor.*   Ensures that the magazine content is accurate and is written correctly.

*Editorial Assistant.*   Performs a wide variety of beginning-level activities—from providing office support to filing to rewriting. The position is a great way to get to know employees and see what different jobs entail.

*Art Director.*    Supervises design and art required for production of the magazine.

*Assistant to the Art Director/Artist.*    Creates and designs graphics and page layouts in preparation for printing.

*Sales Representative.*    Makes presentations to clients to sell advertising space. The sales representative interacts with clients to ensure they are pleased with the results of the advertising project.

*Circulation/Subscription Manager.*    Supervises the planning and financial operations of subscription and newsstand sales.

## NEW MEDIA/MULTIMEDIA

*Consultant.*    Engages in financial, marketing and technology consulting.

*Designer.*    Provides design services for content providers.

*Director.*    Directs the recording of visuals, audio and other media so that they will meet the specific needs of a new media project, such as an Internet sales presentation.

*Producer.*    Plans, budgets, schedules and oversees the often complex requirements of new media projects.

*Programmer.*    Develops programming for online/Internet services.

*Software Developer.*    Develops applications for Internet or CD-ROM products and services.

*Web Master.*    Designs, develops and maintains Web sites.

*Writer.*    Creates concepts and writes scripts for Web-based, interactive or multimedia presentations.

## RADIO STATION

*Station/General Manager.*    Supervises administrative staff, develops station policies, oversees department budgets, keeps current with government and FCC regulations and acts as a liaison to the community. The station manager is usually second-in-command under the owner.

*New Business Development Director.*    Concentrates on creating manufacturer-driven sales partnerships with high-profile, high-traffic organizations—for example, linking advertising sales of a manufactured product with events at a local zoo.

*Sales Representative.*    Sells air time, maintains positive relationships with clients and potential clients, studies market analyses, writes and makes sales presentations.

*National Sales Manager.*   Handles big accounts that come in from other sales offices, usually from cities such as New York, Los Angeles, Chicago, Dallas and Atlanta.

*News Reporter/Writer.*   Writes and reports news gathered from field operations or news wire services.

*Promotions Director.*   Promotes the station and on-air personalities to differentiate the station from competitors and to gain new listeners. This is accomplished through special events, contests and the like.

*Public Service Director.*   Oversees production of public service announcements and placement of all of a station's public service campaigns.

*Traffic/Continuity Manager.*   Prepares the daily log that schedules programming—features, commercials and public service announcements; ensures correct copy in all announcements. This could be divided into two or more positions, depending on the size of the station. Traffic and continuity positions are complicated jobs that require careful attention to detail.

*Station Copy Writer.*   Creates concepts and writes copy for a variety of purposes—commercials, promotions, public service announcements and so on.

*Production Director.*   Responsible for the professional production of commercials and promos. This person records and mixes production elements (such as voice, music and effects), oversees dubbing, works with clients and may write some of the material. Lots of experience is required.

*On-Air Talent.*   Works on-air in specific time periods, reports news or records voice-overs for commercials and promotions; may also act as production director for this work.

*Chief Engineer.*   Participates in the purchase, installation and repair of equipment; ensures that the station operates within proper technical standards; sets up remote broadcasts and coordinates activities with the programming department.

*Producer.*   Every radio show has a producer. The producers of a talk show or morning show lines up guests, schedules and coordinates remotes and keeps things running smoothly.

*Entry-Level Positions.*   Sales assistants enter orders, work on proposals and assist in the day-to-day operations of the sales department. Assistants in the engineering department help with computers, software and broadcast equipment maintenance.

## TELEVISION STATION

*General Manager/Station Manager.* Supervises the day-to-day station operations and plans future operations. All personnel report to the station manager.

*Sales Manager.* Supervises all sales representatives. Since advertising is so important to a station, sales can be a large department.

*Sales Representative.* Sells air time, makes presentations, works with clients and develops new clients.

*Program Director.* Develops and adjusts programming, oversees staff, schedules and budgets for programming.

*Promotions Director.* Promotes the station to differentiate it from the competition and to win new viewers.

*Producer.* Manages the production of a television program or a series of programs. The producer is responsible for content, style, production flow and budgeting.

*Director.* Most work at television stations is multicamera programming conducted in a studio. For these shows, the director establishes camera positions and action sequences, selects which camera shot goes on-air, blocks scripts, works with talent, oversees lighting and is responsible for the look of the program. For programs recorded at remote locations, such as a sports event, the director might work from a remote vehicle to accomplish many of the same operations.

*Technical Director.* Operates the switcher as instructed by the director.

*Videotape Engineer.* Ensures that proper equipment is in place and that it is operating within standards for broadcast.

*Production Assistant.* Runs errands and assists in any way asked. A beginning-level position.

*On-Air Talent.* Acts as news anchor or field reporter, records voice-overs, hosts special programs and attends community events.

*News Crew.* Often called an ENG (electronic news gathering) crew, it consists of a camera operator, sound designer and reporter. One-person crews are now common.

*News Director.* Supervises all aspects of the news operation.

*News Producer.* Usually selects the lead story and the order of news events; is responsible for creating a professional and accurate news program.

*Videotape Editor.*   Edits videotape recorded in the field or downlinked from satellite into news stories and adds voice-overs and music when necessary.

*News Writer.*   Writes news stories, in-depth news specials and related programming as assigned.

*Graphics Artist.*   Works for the art department and creates computer art for news, commercials, promotions and the like.

*Floor Manager.*   Works in the studio, cues talent and acts as liaison between the director and studio personnel.

## VIDEO GAME/INTERACTIVE

*Game Developer.*   Develops game concepts. This could be the company president or a range of staff members.

*3D Animator.*   Creates graphics and animation for use in games.

*Production Manager.*   Oversees live production, art, animation and compositing.

*Computer Programmer.*   Writes and rewrites computer programming for game execution.

*Marketing/Public Relations Director.*   In small companies, many different communications functions are often handled from one office. This person interacts with vendors, the media and customers to promote the company and its products.

*Sales Representative.*   Sells product to various market segments, such as retail outlets and educational distributors.

## VIDEO-PRODUCTION COMPANY

*Producer.*   Manages a production from beginning to end, including content, schedule and budget.

*Director.*   Is responsible for the look of recorded images; blocks scripts for shooting, works with talent, decides composition of images and oversees lighting. This person often works as a freelancer or as part of a small company. Many directors specialize in commercials—even particular types of commercials—industrials or multicamera programs such as sports or soap operas.

*Production Manager.*   Coordinates and schedules the client projects the company is working on.

*Camera Operator.*   Records material on videotape or film for clients. Many shooters also act as directors when shooting nonbroadcast work such as industrial videos.

*Sound Designer.* Coordinates/records music, voice-overs, sound effects for projects; may also act as audio engineer and select/set up audio equipment required for different projects.

*Graphic Artist/Animation Artist.* Creates still and moving images for use in commercials, institutional videos, television/cable programs, CD-ROMs and Web pages.

*Sales Representative.* Makes presentations to clients to gain contract work and submits budgets in conjunction with production manager or producer.

*Writer.* Writes scripts for institutional videos, public service announcements and commercials—if not written by agency personnel.

*Note:* Audio-production facilities have a business structure and work flow similar to that of video-production companies. Those who are interested in music production and the recording of voice-over narration should look into this vibrant part of the industry.

# CONCLUSION

In thinking about and searching for jobs, consider all the possibilities. There are many opportunities other than those at traditional organizations—like television and radio stations. Corporate communications, government and training and development companies complete billions of dollars of communications work annually. What about the video game industry, or any of the growing new media companies supplying Internet communications? Consider the areas with high growth—desktop publishing or public relations. These are all worth exploring.

Second, if you're looking at large companies, be aware that they may be conglomerates encompassing several media fields. AOL/Time Warner is a good example of this, as is Rupert Murdoch's News Corporation. These companies are involved in almost all media and communications fields. AOL/Time Warner is involved in both traditional communications and online services.

Third, a productive way to job hunt is to start with location. If you are moving to a new location, it's worth calling the mayor's office or the local Chamber of Commerce or visiting the appropriate Web sites. These organizations can send you information packets or give you ideas over the phone. Then you can target large organizations and move logically to smaller companies or other areas of interest. If you have contacts in an area, call or write those people to schedule informational interviews. They can tell you about the area you're moving to and about which companies might be hiring. By starting with location, you can proceed in a clear, thorough manner. This strategy will focus your search and is much more likely to turn up opportunities to explore.

It would be easy to claim that there are no secrets to finding jobs or attaining success in the media and communications industries. As you can see, I disagree. Simply put, proper preparation is the secret. I have seen it pay off for many, many people. If you're serious about working in the communications/media fields, you really have no choice. There is intense competition for the best jobs. Preparing yourself while in college can only help you. So . . . you'd better get started.

# APPENDIX:
# SAMPLE RESUMÉS

Students seem to worry about the form of the resumé more than the content. Should I list my education or work experience first? Should this be in bold and that in italics? These questions should be considered, but your time will be better spent on finding a way to present your information clearly, honestly and in a way that puts your best foot forward.

There's nothing you know better than your own life, but what part of it do you put in a resumé? Whenever you have to synthesize material, it's difficult. When it's about yourself, it's even harder. So if you find your first draft to be boring or unfocused, don't worry about it. That's how you start. Just keep working on it, and get some help from classmates and advisors. The resumé is only a snippet of relevant material presented in a way that is easy and interesting to read. If you don't have much relevant work experience and you're just entering the job market, there's only one thing you can do about it—go get the experience.

You will find eight sample student resumés in this appendix. Each resumé was written for a different area of communications. Note that these resumés have different formats, but each emphasizes work experiences, internships, community involvement and awards. Each one also has a single focus and a pleasing look, and is easy for an employer to read—even skim. Some of the resumés are longer than others. If you have an exceptional story to tell from your college and related experiences, tell it. You can always shorten your resumé later. Even with that said, note that all but two of the resumés included here fit on one page.

Part of what keeps a resumé tightly focused is what you leave out. Hobbies, for example, are not normally listed. Some professionals recommend including a job objective, but I find them difficult to write. They often seem to miss the mark because they're too general, too specific or trite. A job objective can be included in your cover letter. Cover letters are extremely important. Excellent samples of cover letters can be found in *200 Letters for Job Hunters,* by William S. Frank. This book and other helpful references are listed in the Additional Resources section at the back of the book.

Finally, as you're reading the resumés on the following pages, take note of the kinds of experiences these students sought during their college years. Now their hard work is paying off and giving them resumés that will attract attention and land job interviews.

## PUBLIC RELATIONS

# Joseph P. Field

12 Highland Avenue    McDonald, PA 15057    (412) 555-0102

EDUCATION:

**Bachelor of Arts**, Public Relations    2001
**Robert Morris College**   Moon Township, PA 15108
Graduated Magna Cum Laude

- Alpha Chi National Scholarship Society member
- Vice President for Commuter Affairs

AWARDS:

**Telly** (Silver),   **CINDY** (Finalist),   **New York Festivals** (Finalist)

COMMUNICATION
EXPERIENCE:

*Intern*: **The White House**, Office of the Press Secretary    2000

- Helped prepare daily press briefings, news releases, and television interviews
- Acted as a liaison between the national press corps and senior White House staff members
- Directed the inquiries of journalists to the appropriate Administration source
- Proofed/edited official documents before their release

**Public Relations Coordinator**, RMC-TV    2000

- Responsible for designing and implementing promotional activities
- Wrote a grant-winning proposal for a national video production sponsored by the Association of College and University Housing Officers International (ACUHO-I)
- Started weekly RMC-TV "Studio Notes" column in college newspaper
- Developed advertising campaign to promote new season of programming
- Created new logo and station identity program

*Intern*: **Academic Media Center**, Robert Morris College   1999-2000

- Participated in preproduction planning
- Scripted and produced public service announcements for the Pittsburgh Airport Area Chamber of Commerce
- Assistant directed Robert Morris Colonials football broadcasts

**Member**: Public Relations Society of America
REFERENCES AVAILABLE UPON REQUEST

## CORPORATE COMMUNICATIONS

---

### *Heather Long*
3412 Valley Drive
Los Angeles, CA 90024
(310) 555-6554

---

**EDUCATION**

*San Francisco State College*      August 1998-December 2000
Bachelor of Science in Communications Management

Palo Alto Business School      July 1996-October 1997
Associate Degree in Business Administration

**EXPERIENCE**

*Sun Microsystems* - Intern
- Wrote training brochures
- Assisted in developing new employee orientation

*Trak Auto*      1997-Present
Cashier: Answer phones, provide customer service, sell merchandise, stock shelves, operate register and parts computer.

*Olsten Staffing Service*      1998-Present
Temporary positions for various companies.
General duties: Answer phone, data entry, photocopy, complete any secretarial duties as needed.

*Diamond Group, Inc.*      1997-1998
Administrative Assistant: answered phones, filed, typed, computed payroll in Lotus 123r3, prepared paychecks for distribution, created quarter payroll reports, formulated AIA and Invoices for billings, completed paperwork for worker's compensation and child support, completed any secretarial duties as needed.

**ACHIEVEMENTS**

Palo Alto Transfer Scholarship
Volunteered 72 hours at Country Meadows Nursing Home
Volunteered two years for Habitat for Humanity

**COMPUTER**
**SKILLS**

| dBase III Plus | Lotus 123r3 | WordPerfect |
| Microsoft Word | Accurate Typing | Media Writing Abilities |
| Computing Payroll | Telephone Skills | |

*REFERENCES AVAILABLE UPON REQUEST*

## GRAPHIC ARTS/ANIMATOR

■■■■■■■■■ ■■■■■■■■■■■■■■■■■■■■ ■■■■■■■■■■■■■

# SCOTT JACKSON

312 Overview Road                                          East Lansing, MI 48824
                         (517) 555-2212

■■■■■■■■■ ■■■■■■■■■■■■■■■■■■■■ ■■■■■■■■■■■■■

**Education**
Bachelor of Science in Communications Mass Media                      May 1996
Michigan State University

**Career Related Skills**
Computer graphic 3D/2D animation, CAD modeling, special video processing effects, layout/design and illustration for multimedia and print purposes

**Professional Experience**
■ Creative Imaging                                           1999-Present
<u>Position</u>: Owner/Operator - Independent graphics and multimedia servicing. Provides 3D/2D computer animation, roto-scoping, graphic video processing and effects, Web page design, HTML programming and desktop publishing/layout and design for external clients.

■ JPL Productions                                           1997-1999
<u>Position</u>: Art Director/Graphic Artist - responsible for coordinating and creating graphics with both in-house and external clients. Specialized in 3D/2D computer animation, graphic video processing and effects and layout/design for broadcast television, video and film.

■ WPMI-TV PBS                                               1996-1997
<u>Position</u>: Graphics/Production Technician - Worked with graphics department providing design for both national and local broadcast programs. Also provided control room and remote graphics support.

**Honors and Awards**
■ Music Television Networks (MTV)                                      1994
$1,000.00 awarded for an independent music video production entry noted for its graphic video processing and airing nationally.

■ College and Universities Public Relations Association of PA Media Award        1995
$1,500.00 awarded for an independent video production entry noted for its graphic video processing and special effects. This production entitled "World Drug War I" competed with all college and university student media productions in the state of Pennsylvania.

■ Mass Media Award                                           1995
Presented for an independent student production entitled "Creativity," which expressed the new-found

## GRAPHIC ARTS/ANIMATOR (*CONT.*)

realm of production capabilities and the incorporation of the computer for graphics production servicing.

■ Addy Awards                                                                                          1996
Silver Addy awarded to JPL Productions for a thirty-second national animation entitled "We All Live Downstream," which was created for the Chesapeake Bay Foundation and displayed both live video rotoscoping with an animated re-creation of a virtual fly-through of the surrounding streams and rivers flowing into the Chesapeake Bay region.

■ Member: International Television and Video Association (ITVA)

**Military Experience**
■ United States Army Reserves                                                            1988-1992
Headquarters Company 315th Combat Engineer Group
New Cumberland Army Depot, New Cumberland, PA

Position: 31 Kilo communications Combat Engineer - Responsible for establishing and maintaining communications in the field and with an aviation group.

# RADIO

---

## ANTHONY G. CANTINI

22 Thompson Road
Erie, PA 16208
(814) 555-5451

---

**EDUCATION:**

Allegheny College: Meadville, PA 16335
Bachelor of Arts in Media Production, May 1998

**COMMUNICATIONS EXPERIENCE:**

WBPA 29   Pittsburgh, PA   1999 - Present
WTWB 19   Johnstown, PA

Master Control Technician/Production Editor: responsible for on-air programming, satellite feeds, editing, daily maintenance of equipment and commercial traffic.

WDUQ 90.5   Pittsburgh, PA   1996 - Present

Host: *Jazz in the Afternoon*, 1996 - 1998; Master of Ceremonies for remote broadcasts and events, 1997 - present; Technical Assistant for remote broadcasts, 1996 - present.

WAAA 90.3   Meadville, PA   1993-1996

General Manager: Supervised over 100 volunteers a semester over two years. Strengthened relations with administration and Communication Arts Department. Spearheaded FCC application for power increase. Oversaw reorganization of Executive Board and personnel training.

Director: Served as Director of the following posts: news, music, production and engineering.

**ACTIVITIES:**

Pittsburgh Irish Festival   1997 - Present

Master of Ceremonies, Stage Director: 1998 Irish Festival, 1998 St. Patrick's Day Celebration.

Assistant Stage Director, Assistant Sound Technician: 1997 Irish Festival.

**MEMBER:**

National Association of Radio Broadcasters

References Supplied Upon Request

## TELEVISION PRODUCER

# James Tabor
### 239 Lakeside Lane   Memphis, TN 37217
### (615) 555-6631

*Education*   Degree: BS/BA   Major: Communications Management   Major GPA: 3.8

*Media Work*   Academic Media Center, University of Memphis   1999 - Present
*Experience*   ◆   Station Manager of AMC-TV, Channel 10
◆   Producer and writer of a national video for the Association of College and Universities Housing Officers International (ACUHO-I)
◆   Producer of Front & Center, a half-hour movie review program
◆   Co-producer and writer of a regional video for the National Teacher's Training Institute for WQED, Channel 13
◆   P.A. for location shoot in Boston, MA, to cover the "Year 2000 Initiative"
◆   Cablecasting Supervisor for the 1996 winter semester for Channel 10
◆   Various crew positions including director, technical director, camera operator and graphics operator

New Productions (Summer 1999)
501 Baum Blvd.  Memphis, TN 37217
*Intern*
◆   Clientele - AAA, Idlewild Park, BNAC and Iron City
◆   Experience in technical operations, location shooting skills, nonlinear editing and agency-client relationships

*Other Work*   Ray's Clothing & Sporting Goods (1999 - Present)
*Experience*   Robinson Town Center, Memphis, TN 37217
*Clothing sales associate*
◆   Assist customers on the sales floor
◆   Merchandise new items onto the sales floor and sign sale items

Dairy Queen (1995 - 1999)
Highway 101, Eugene, TN 37307
*Assistant Manager*
◆   Managed all employees on shifts along with closing registers and the store
◆   Assisted customers and handled customer problems

*Awards &*   2001 Outstanding Communications Management Student of the Year
*Honors*   2001 Academic Media Center Student of the Year
2001 Who's Who Among American Universities and Colleges
Repeated Dean's List student

*References supplied upon request*

## TEACHING

# Erin Smith

2458 Alexander Manor                                    Albion, OH 43952
(614) 555-7200

**Education:**  Bachelor of Arts, English & Communications Education. GPA: 3.94  May 2001
Pennsylvania State Certification in English Education and Communications
(Video Production) Education.
Robert Morris College, Moon Township, PA

**Experience:**  **Student Teacher,** West Allegheny High School, Fall 2000.
Responsible for creating and delivering curriculum for English and Videography
Classes.
Assumed all planning, grading and teaching responsibilities of cooperating
teacher.
Acquired valuable presentation and social skills interacting with students, faculty
and administration. Demonstrated initiative and creativity through the following
projects:
• created a Video Scrapbook project for students surrounding their participation in
  President Clinton's visit to the area
• arranged an interview with anchor, to help students learn valuable interviewing
  techniques
• organized a field trip to TV studio so students could create their own studio
  production
• intertwined the use of video in my English classrooms by having students create
  a mini-screenplay extending "Walter Mitty's" daydreams
• Used creative resources to teach English students how to write a proper
  business letter

**Cafe Associate,** Barnes and Noble Bookseller, April 2000 to present.
Responsible for giving quality customer service and maintenance of cafe
facilities. Asked to instruct new employees on proper procedures.

**Business Manager,** TVT, Teacher of Television and Video Consortium, 2000.
Organized events for the annual TVT Student Festival, which included mailing,
member contact and program coordination. Contributed articles to the TVT
newsletter and assisted in publication for distribution. Used document design to
create an official brochure for the TVT organization.

**Assistant Business Manager,** Franchise Specialist Inc., May 1999 to May 2000.
Part-time assistant responsible for conducting sales using telemarketing strategies
to connect the client with the FSI owner. Redesigned the official letters sent to all
potential clients and created the first client portfolio of the company.

**Master Teacher,** NTTI, National Teachers Training Institute, Nov. 1999.
Presented with members of the Robert Morris College Academic Media Center at
Carnegie Science Center in Pittsburgh, PA. Discussed the value of teaching video

## TEACHING (*CONT.*)

production and the need for technological exposure in the classroom. Introduced ideas for interdisciplinary lessons and projects.

*Activities:*    **Ambassador of Robert Morris College**
One of twenty-five members selected through an interview process to represent and serve the college at alumni functions. Must have a GPA of 3.0 or above and demonstrate strong leadership and communication abilities to be considered for selection.

**Western Region Secretary, Student Pennsylvania State Education Association**
Acted as a communication link between local chapters and region president. Also, acting President of the Robert Morris College chapter. Responsible for organizing meetings and providing practical services for education majors on campus.

**Co-Captain, Robert Morris Cheerleading Squad** (1997-1999)
Supervised 16-member co-ed squad. Assisted in curriculum development for National Competitions held in Dallas, Texas.

**Cameron Coca-Cola Senior Leadership Award**, 2001
Awarded to outstanding seniors for extraordinary efforts and participation in campus life. Recommendations made by students or faculty members.

**Who's Who in American College Students**, 2001
Awarded to those with superior academic and leadership abilities.

**English Student of the Year**, 2000
Awarded to an exemplary English major. Selected by faculty members taking GPA and leadership qualities into consideration.

**Alpha Chi Honor Society**
Awarded to those who kept above a 3.5 GPA for five consecutive semesters.

**Academic and Leadership Scholarship Recipient**
Awarded to students who show exceptional leadership abilities in high school.

**Deans List Honors**
Received above a 3.5 GPA during all eight semesters

*Computer*     WordPerfect           Microsoft Word
*Knowledge:*    Lotus 1-2-3           PowerPoint

References supplied upon request.

**JOURNALISM**

# Carey Wells
### 220 Ocean Drive
### San Diego, CA  92113
### 213-555-2388

EDUCATION:

B.A. in Journalism   2001
University of California at San Diego

Minor in Business Management
Concentration in Business Writing

EXPERIENCE:

Communications

REPORTER • *San Diego Business Weekly* • Summer Position • 2000

Reported news, conducted interviews, covered town meetings, business
events, particularly high-tech, and wrote articles.

ASSISTANT EDITOR  •  *University Times*  •  1999-2001
Assigned articles, oversaw production and sales.

Activities

COORDINATOR • ABC Walk for the Cure • San Diego  •  1998-2001

VOLUNTEER • Woods Home for the Elderly • San Diego •  2000
Helped patients write correspondence

Member

American Society of Journalists and Authors

References

Available upon request

## ADVERTISING

# Tiffany Flaherty
354 Highland Avenue
New Orleans, LA 70127
(504) 555-8778

### EDUCATION

| | | |
|---|---|---|
| degree: | BA in Advertising | 2001 |
| | University of New Orleans | |
| minor: | Psychology | |
| course work: | Advertising, Writing for Media, TV Production, Radio Production | |

accomplishments:   Developed multimedia ad campaign for insurance company
Participated in writing/design of press kit for radio station
Weekend News Broadcaster - WTDC 104.9

### EXPERIENCE

advertising:   Intern                                    Fall 2000
New Works Agency, Auburn, LA
Assisted broadcast producer with scheduling and producing
commercials on film and videotape

general:   Supervisor/Cashier/Waitress          1998-2000
Bob's Restaurant, Blossom, LA
Supervised other servers, handled cash register, counted receipts and
waited on patrons

### ACTIVITIES

Ran two track events on varsity track squad. Learned strong work ethic
and value of determination

### MEMBER

Advertising Club of New Orleans

References available upon request

# ADDITIONAL RESOURCES

Bob Adams, Inc., eds. *The Adams Jobs Almanac 1998*. Holbrook, MA: Adams Publishing, 1997.

Bolles, Richard. *What Color Is Your Parachute? 1997: A Practical Manual for Job-Hunters and Career-Changers*. Berkeley, CA: Ten Speed Press, 1997.

Bouchard, Jerry. *Graduating to the 9 to 5 World*. Woodbridge, VA: Impact Publications, 1991.

Camenson, Blythe. *Great Jobs for Communications Majors*. Lincolnwood, IL: VGM Career Horizons, 1995.

Career Associates. *Career Choices Encyclopedia*. New York: Walker and Co., 1986.

Carter, Carol. *Majoring in the Rest of Your Life: Career Secrets for College Students*. New York: Noonday Press, 1995.

Cohen, William A. *The Student's Guide to Finding a Superior Job*. 2nd ed. San Diego: Pfieffer & Co., 1993.

Farris, Linda Guess. *Television Careers: A Guide to Breaking and Entering*. Fairfax, CA: Buy the Book Enterprises, 1995.

Fisher, Helen S. *American Salaries and Wages Survey*. 3rd ed. New York: Gale Research, 1995.

Fournier, Myra, and Jeffrey Spin. *Encyclopedia of Job-Winning Resumes*. Ridgefield, CT: Round Lake Publishing, 1993.

Frank, William S. *200 Letters for Job Hunters*. Berkeley, CA: Ten Speed Press, 1993.

Fry, Ron. *Your First Job: For Students and Anyone Preparing to Enter Today's Tough Job Market*. 2nd ed. Hawthorne, NJ: Career Press, 1993.

Gould, Jay R., and Wayne A. Losano. *Opportunities in Technical Writing and Communications Careers*. Lincolnwood, IL: VGM Career Horizons, 1994.

Gouldberg, Jan. *Real People Working in Communications*. Lincolnwood, IL: VGM Career Horizons, 1997.

Graber, Steven. *The Everything Cover Letter Book*. Holbrook: Adams Media, 2000.

Holzaepfel, Cherl, ed. *Careers in Multimedia: A Comprehensive Guide to the World of Interactive Media Development.* Emeryville, CA: Ziff-Davis Press, 1995.

Kador, John. *Internet Jobs!* New York: McGraw-Hill, 2000.

Kanter, Rosabeth Moss. Introduction to *The Best Companies for Minorities,* by Lawrence Otis Graham. New York: Plume, 1993.

Kleiman, Carol. *The 100 Best Jobs for the 1990's and Beyond.* Chicago, IL: Dearborn Financial Publishing, 1992.

Krantz, Les. *The Wall Street Journal National Business Employment Weekly: Jobs Rated Almanac.* 3rd ed. New York: John Wiley & Sons, 1995.

Leape, Martha, and Susan M. Vacca. *The Harvard Guide to Careers.* Cambridge, MA: Harvard University Press, 1995.

LeCompte, Michelle, ed. *Job Hunter's Sourcebook.* 3rd ed. New York: Gale Research, 1996.

Morgan, Bradley J., and Joseph Palmisano, eds. *Film and Video Career Directory: A Practical, One-Step Guide to Getting a Job in Film and Video.* New York: Gale Research, 1994.

*National Business Employment Weekly: Premier Guides.* New York: John Wiley & Sons, 1994. Premier Guides Series includes five books on Networking, Resumés, Interviewing, Cover Letters, and Alternative Careers.

Oldman, Mark and Samer Hamadeh. *The Internship Bible: 2001 Edition.* New York: Random House, 2001.

Rich, Carole. *Creating Online Media: A Guide to Research, Writing and Design on the Internet.* Boston: McGraw-Hill College, 1999.

Richardson, Bradley G. *Jobsmarts for Twentysomethings.* New York: Vintage Books, 1995.

Schmidt, Robert. *The National Jobline Directory.* Holbrook, MA: Adams Publishing, 1994.

Sherman, Aliza. *Cybergrrl@work: Tips and Inspiration for the Professional You.* New York: Berkley Books, 2001.

U.S. Bureau of Labor Statistics. *Occupational Projections and Training Data.* Washington, DC: Government Printing Office, 1994.

U.S. Department of Labor. *Occupational Outlook Handbook.* Washington, DC: Government Printing Office, 1996–97.

Weddle, Peter D. *Weddle's Job-Seeker's Guide to Employment Web Sites 2001.* New York: AMACOM, 2001.

Williams, Marcia P., and Sue A. Cubbage. *The 1997 National Job Hotline Directory.* New York: McGraw-Hill, 1997.

Wright, John W. *The American Almanac of Jobs and Salaries.* New York: Avon Books, 1996.

# INDEX